**GoodFood**

# 101 MEDITERRANEAN DISHES

10 9 8 7 6 5 4

Published in 2008 by BBC Books,
an imprint of Ebury Publishing
A Random House Group Company

The Random House Group Limited
Reg. No. 954009

Addresses for companies within the
Random House Group can be found at
www.randomhouse.co.uk

A CIP catalogue record for this book is
available from the British Library.

The Random House Group Limited supports
The Forest Stewardship Council (FSC), the
leading international forest certification organization.
All our titles that are printed on Greenpeace
approved FSC certified paper carry the FSC logo.
Our paper procurement policy can be found at
www.rbooks.co.uk/environment

To buy books by your favourite authors and
register for offers visit www.rbooks.co.uk

Printed and bound by Firmengruppe APPL,
aprinta druck, Wemding, Germany
Colour origination by Dot Gradations Ltd, UK

Commissioning Editor: Lorna Russell
Project Editor: Laura Higginson
Designer: Annette Peppis
Jacket Design: Kathryn Gammon
Production: David Brimble
Picture Researchers: Gabby Harrington
and Natalie Lief

ISBN: 9781846074257

# GoodFood

# 101 MEDITERRANEAN DISHES
## TRIED-AND-TESTED RECIPES

Editor
**Angela Nilsen**

# Contents

# Introduction

As the availability and choice of Mediterranean ingredients becomes more and more plentiful – from fruity olive oils and roasted vegetables to couscous, flavoursome cheeses and fancy-shaped pastas and breads – experiencing the benefits and enjoyment of Mediterranean cooking at home couldn't be easier.

Flavours from cuisines such as Italian, Spanish, Greek, North African are big favourites with the *Good Food* team, and many of the recipes in *BBC Good Food Magazine* reflect the versatility of these cuisines. They are often first choice when it comes to using grilled meats, fish and seafood for speedy, healthy suppers for the family or relaxed alfresco menus for friends – all of which you'll find in this book. To complete this special collection, there are recipes that make the most of sea-sonal ingredients – with ideas for colourful vegetable dishes and salads, summery soups, juicy fruit tarts and ices and as well as simple tapas and meze dishes.

Each recipe comes complete with a nutritional breakdown, so you can see just how healthy it is, and a thorough testing in the *Good Food* kitchen assures its delicious taste. So read on and enjoy these recipes from sunny climes, and enter a world of stress-free cooking all year round.

Angela Nilsen
*BBC Good Food Magazine*

# Notes and Conversion tables

## NOTES ON THE RECIPES
• Eggs are large in the UK and Australia unless stated otherwise.
• Wash all fresh produce before preparation.
• Recipes contain nutritional analyses for 'sugar', which means the total sugar content including all natural sugars in the ingredients unless otherwise stated.

## OVEN TEMPERATURES

| Gas | °C | Fan °C | °F | Oven temp. |
|-----|-----|--------|-----|----------------|
| ¼ | 110 | 90 | 225 | Very cool |
| ½ | 120 | 100 | 250 | Very cool |
| 1 | 140 | 120 | 275 | Cool or slow |
| 2 | 150 | 130 | 300 | Cool or slow |
| 3 | 160 | 140 | 325 | Warm |
| 4 | 180 | 160 | 350 | Moderate |
| 5 | 190 | 170 | 375 | Moderately hot |
| 6 | 200 | 180 | 400 | Fairly hot |
| 7 | 220 | 200 | 425 | Hot |
| 8 | 230 | 210 | 450 | Very hot |
| 9 | 240 | 220 | 475 | Very hot |

## APPROXIMATE WEIGHT CONVERSIONS
• All the recipes in this book list both imperial and metric measurements. Conversions are approximate and have been rounded up or down. Follow one set of measurements only; do not mix the two.
• Cup measurements, which are used by cooks in Australia and America, have not been listed here as they vary from ingredient to ingredient. Please use kitchen scales to measure dry/solid ingredients.

## SPOON MEASURES

Spoon measurements are level unless otherwise specified.

- 1 teaspoon = 5ml
- 1 tablespoon = 15ml
- 1 Australian tablespoon = 20ml (cooks in Australia should measure 3 teaspoons where 1 tablespoon is specified in a recipe)

## APPROXIMATE LIQUID CONVERSIONS

| metric | imperial | AUS | US |
| --- | --- | --- | --- |
| 50ml | 2fl oz | ¼ cup | ¼ cup |
| 125ml | 4fl oz | ½ cup | ½ cup |
| 175ml | 6fl oz | ¾ cup | ¾ cup |
| 225ml | 8fl oz | 1 cup | 1 cup |
| 300ml | 10fl oz/½ pint | ½ pint | 1¼ cups |
| 450ml | 16fl oz | 2 cups | 2 cups/1 pint |
| 600ml | 20fl oz/1 pint | 1 pint | 2½ cups |
| 1 litre | 35fl oz/1¾ pints | 1¾ pints | 1 quart |

If you can't get hold of tinned tomatoes with paprika, just use a can of plain chopped tomatoes and add a pinch of hot paprika instead.

# Spinach and Feta Cannelloni

4 large sheets no-pre-cook lasagne
1kg/2lb 4oz frozen spinach, defrosted
200g pack low-fat feta
generous grating fresh nutmeg
large handful of olives, pitted and chopped
1 tbsp capers, rinsed
400g can chopped tomatoes
25g/1oz Parmesan, grated

Takes 35 minutes, plus thawing
Serves 4

1  Pre-heat the oven to 200°C/Gas 6/fan 180°C. Put the lasagne sheets in a large bowl and cover with boiling water. Soak for 5 minutes or prepare according to the packet instructions.

2  Meanwhile, squeeze as much water as possible from the spinach then mix with the feta, nutmeg and some seasoning. Drain the pasta then cut each sheet in half vertically. Spoon four tablespoons of the filling along the centre of each half, then roll up to enclose. Place in a lightly oiled baking dish.

3  Mix the olives, capers and tomatoes together in a bowl, season, then spoon over the cannelloni. Sprinkle with Parmesan, cover with foil, then bake for 20 minutes.

• Per serving 274 kcalories, protein 22g, carbohydrate 22g, fat 12g, saturated fat 5g, fibre 8g, sugar 7g, salt 3.54g

For a more hearty meal, add some potatoes. Peel and cut a medium potato into eight wedges and roast with the chicken and peppers.

# One-pan Summer Chicken

2 red peppers
large handfuls of basil leaves, torn
1 plump garlic clove, sliced
2 plum tomatoes, halved
2 chicken leg quarters
2 tbsp extra virgin olive oil
410g can butter beans, drained and rinsed

Takes 35–40 minutes • Serves 2

1 Pre-heat the oven to 220°C/Gas 7/fan 200°C. Cut the peppers in half lengthways and scoop out the seeds and white membrane. Ttry to keep the stalk attached. Stuff each pepper half with basil (but don't use it all), the garlic and a tomato half.
2 Place the stuffed peppers alongside the chicken in a roasting tin. Drizzle oil over everything and season. Roast for 25–30 minutes until the chicken is golden and the peppers have softened and wrinkled. Lift out on to a plate, tipping the peppers so that the juice drains back into the roasting tin.
3 Place the tin over a low flame and add a little water and the beans and heat through. Stir in the remaining basil and serve with the chicken and peppers.

• Per serving 620 kcalories, protein 42g, carbohydrate 29g. fat 38g, saturated fat 10g, fibre 9g, sugar 13g, salt 1.49g

It's important to use a good-quality stock in this dish – so choose a decent one that's not too salty.

# Roasted Pepper and Mascarpone Risotto

50g/2oz unsalted butter
1 small onion, peeled and finely chopped
1 garlic clove, crushed
2 red or yellow roasted peppers from a jar, sliced
175g/6oz risotto rice, such as arborio
1 litre/1¾ pints vegetable or chicken stock, kept just below boiling point in a pan
50g/2oz diced pancetta
1 tbsp olive oil
2 tbsp finely chopped flatleaf parsley
3 tbsp mascarpone cheese
50g/2oz freshly grated Parmesan, plus extra to serve
1 tbsp snipped fresh chives, for garnishing

Takes 1–1¼ hours • Serves 2

1  Melt the butter in a large, heavy-bottomed pan. Fry the onion gently for 10 minutes until soft. Add the garlic and three-quarters of the peppers. Stir gently over a low heat, for 3 minutes, then add the rice. Stir until the grains are coated and toasted all over, for about 5 minutes. Add a ladleful of hot stock and stir.
2  Continue slowly adding stock and stirring in until the grains are plump and swollen. Meanwhile, in a separate pan, fry the pancetta in olive oil until it is brown and crisp.
3  When the rice is just chewy, take it off the heat and stir in seasoning plus the remaining ingredients. Cover it and let it stand for about 3 minutes before spooning on to serving plates. Garnish with the chives and offer extra Parmesan at the table.

• Per serving 895 kcalories, protein 27g, carbohydrate 83g, fat 53g, saturated fat 28g, fibre 5g, added sugar none, salt 3.33g

Once you've tasted delicious home-made pizza, you won't be ordering one ever again.

# Pizza

## FOR THE BASE
300g/10oz strong bread flour
1 tsp instant yeast (from a sachet or a tub)
1 tsp salt
1 tbsp olive oil, plus extra for drizzling

## FOR THE TOMATO SAUCE
100ml/3½ fl oz passata
handful of fresh basil or 1 tsp dried
1 garlic clove, crushed

## FOR THE TOPPING
125g ball mozzarella, sliced
handful grated or shaved Parmesan
handful of cherry tomatoes, halved

## TO FINISH
handful of basil leaves

Takes 35 minutes • Makes 2 pizzas, serves 4

1  Mix the flour, yeast and salt in a bowl. Stir in 200ml/7fl oz warm water and the olive oil to give a soft, fairly wet dough. Knead on a lightly floured surface for 5 minutes. Cover and set aside while you make the sauce. Mix the passata, basil and garlic, season to taste. Let stand at room temperature.

2  Shape the dough into two balls. On a floured surface, roll the dough into 25cm/10in rounds. Put them on floured baking sheets.

3  Pre-heat the oven to 240°C/Gas 9/fan 220°C. Put a baking sheet in the oven on the top shelf. Smooth sauce over the bases. Scatter with the cheese, tomatoes, drizzle with olive oil and season. Put one pizza, on its baking sheet, on top of the pre-heated sheet. Bake for 8–10 minutes until crisp. Repeat with the remaining pizza.

• Per serving 431 kcalories, protein 19g, carbohydrate 59g, fat 15g, saturated fat 7g, fibre 3g, sugar 2g, salt 1.87g

A wonderfully simple but tasty fish dish. Serve with crusty bread to mop up the sauce.

# Fish with Black Olives and Tomatoes

2 tbsp olive oil
1 onion, peeled and roughly chopped
¼ tsp chilli powder (optional)
400g can chopped tomatoes
1 tbsp tomato purée
½ tsp dried oregano
175g/6oz black olives, pitted
4 boneless white fish fillets such as
Icelandic cod or hoki
(about 175g/6oz each)
chopped fresh flatleaf parsley,
to garnish
1 lemon, cut into wedges, to serve

Takes 25–30 minutes • Serves 4

1  Pre-heat the oven to 200°C/Gas 6/fan 180°C. Heat one tablespoon of the oil in an ovenproof pan on the hob. Add the onion and chilli, if using, and cook for a few minutes, stirring occasionally. Add the tomatoes, tomato purée, oregano and some salt and pepper. Bring to the boil then add the olives.
2  Put the fish, skin-side down, on to the sauce and drizzle over the remaining oil. Bake, uncovered, in the oven for 15 minutes until the fish is cooked. Sprinkle with chopped parsley and serve with lemon wedges to squeeze over the fish.

• Per portion 286 kcalories, protein 34.1g, carbohydrate 5.6g, fat 14.3g, saturated fat 1.9g, fibre 3.6g, sugar 4.4g, salt 1.16g

A new twist on a classic recipe that's ideal for non-meat eaters.

# Italian Tuna Balls

2 x160g cans tuna in sunflower
or olive oil, drained
(reserve a little oil)
small handful of pine nuts
freshly grated zest 1 lemon
small handful of parsley leaves,
roughly chopped
50g/2oz fresh breadcrumbs
1 egg, beaten
400g/14oz spaghetti
500g jar tomato pasta sauce

Takes 20 minutes • Serves 4

1  Flake the tuna into a bowl, then tip in the pine nuts, lemon zest, parsley, breadcrumbs and egg. Season and mix together with your hands until completely combined.
2  Roll the mix into 12 walnut-sized balls. Put a large pan of salted water on to boil, then cook the spaghetti according to the packet instructions.
3  Heat a little of the tuna oil in a large, non-stick frying pan, then fry the tuna balls for 5 minutes, turning every minute or so until completely golden. Drain on kitchen paper. Heat the tomato sauce, then toss together with the pasta and tuna balls.

• Per serving 594 kcalories, protein 35g, carbohydrate 92g, fat 12g, saturated fat 2g, fibre 4g, sugar 8g, salt 1.42g

A quick supper for a busy weeknight. To make it vegetarian, just leave out the bacon.

# Quick Veg and Soft Cheese Frittata

100g/4oz lardons or chopped
streaky bacon
1 tbsp olive oil
2 large courgettes, cut into chunks
350g/12oz frozen sweetcorn
400g/14oz frozen spinach, defrosted
and drained
8 eggs
150g pack full or medium fat soft
cheese with garlic and herbs
green salad, to serve

Takes 30 minutes, plus defrosting
Serves 4

1 Fry the lardons or bacon in the oil in a large, non-stick frying pan until starting to brown. Stir in the courgettes then fry for a couple of minutes until they begin to soften. Add the sweetcorn and spinach, season if you like, then heat through.

2 Heat the grill to medium. Beat the eggs and pour over the vegetables. Crumble over the cheese then cook gently until the egg has just set around the edges, about 5 minutes.

3 Slide the frittata under the grill and cook it until the egg is set and the top is lightly browned. Cut into wedges and serve with a simple green salad.

• Per serving 540 kcalories, protein 29g, carbohydrate 18g, fat 40g, saturated fat 16g, fibre 4g, sugar 5g, salt 1.62g

As a variation, lay torn strips of prosciutto under the peppers
and scatter the baked tart with toasted pine nuts.

# Tomato and Mozzarella Tart with Roast Peppers

375g pack ready-rolled puff pastry
85g/3oz Parmesan, coarsely grated
450g jar whole roasted red peppers
olive oil, for brushing and drizzling
(basil oil is good)
2 x 125g packs mozzarella balls,
drained
4–5 medium-large ripe tomatoes,
sliced
basil leaves, for scattering

Takes 25–30 minutes • Serves 6

1  Put a baking sheet in the oven and pre-heat to 220°C/Gas 7/fan 200°C. Use the pastry to line a rectangular tin 20 x 30cm/8 x 12in. Prick the base lightly with a fork.
2  Scatter the Parmesan over the pastry base. Drain the peppers. Lay the whole peppers widthways across the pastry base. If the peppers aren't in oil, brush a little over them and the pastry and season. Bake for about 15 minutes until the pastry is puffy and golden.
3  Slice the mozzarella. Lay alternating, slightly overlapping lines of tomato and mozzarella over the peppers. Drizzle with oil, scatter with basil leaves and an extra grinding of black pepper, then serve while the pastry is still warm.

• Per serving 540 kcalories, protein 23g, carbohydrate 29g, fat 38g, saturated fat 17g, fibre 2g, added sugar 0g, salt 2.54g

This is a lower fat version of the classic dish, as softening the aubergine in the microwave, instead of frying it, reduces the amount of oil it usually soaks up.

# Must-make Moussaka

500g/1lb 2oz lean minced beef
1 large aubergine
150g carton 0% thick Greek yoghurt
1 egg, beaten
3 tbsp of finely grated Parmesan
400g can chopped tomatoes with garlic and herbs
4 tbsp sun-dried tomato purée
400g/14oz leftover boiled potatoes
(or 350g/12oz uncooked, boiled)

Takes 30 minutes • Serves 4

1  Heat the grill to high. Brown the beef in a deep, ovenproof frying pan over a high heat for 5 minutes.

2  Meanwhile, prick the aubergine with a fork (so it doesn't burst), then microwave on High for 3–5 minutes until soft. Mix the yoghurt, egg and Parmesan together, then add a little seasoning.

3  Stir in the tomatoes, purée and potatoes with the beef plus some seasoning then heat through. Smooth the surface of the beef mixture with the back of a spoon, then slice the cooked aubergine and arrange on top. Pour the yoghurt mixture over the aubergines, smooth out evenly, then grill until the topping has set and turned golden.

• Per serving 342 kcalories, protein 41g, carbohydrate 25g, fat 9g, saturated fat 4g, fibre 4g, sugar 6g, salt 0.97g

You can make this a veggie pizza by replacing the tuna with marinated artichokes or chargrilled peppers or aubergines from a jar from the deli counter.

# Ten-minute Tuna Pizza

23cm/9in thin-crust pizza base
1 tbsp tomato purée
1 garlic clove, peeled and sliced
handful of pitted black olives
large of handful cherry tomatoes, halved
1 tbsp olive oil, for drizzling
1 tbsp capers, drained
200g can tuna in brine, drained and flaked
handful of basil leaves

Takes 15–20 minutes • Serves 2

1  Pre-heat the oven to 230°C/Gas 8/fan 210°C. Spread the pizza base with tomato purée. Scatter over the garlic, olives, tomatoes and half the oil.
2  Bake for 10 minutes until the tomatoes start to colour and the base is crisp.
3  Remove from the oven, sprinkle over the capers, tuna and basil, drizzle with remaining oil, then serve.

• Per serving 322 kcalories, protein 25g, carbohydrate 38g, fat 9g, saturated fat 2g, fibre 2g, sugar 1g, salt 2.65g

A fabulously simple and tasty supper to make when time is short.
Serve with a fresh green salad.

# Couscous with Chorizo and Chickpeas

250g/9oz couscous
300ml/½ pint boiling vegetable stock
2 tbsp olive oil
200g/8oz sliced chorizo
1 onion, peeled and sliced
1 tsp paprika
400g can chickpeas, drained
425ml/¾ pint chicken stock
chopped fresh parsley, to serve

Takes 25–30 minutes • Serves 4

1  Put the couscous into a large bowl. Pour over the boiling stock and stir. Cover with a plate or cling film and leave to stand for 5 minutes until all the liquid has been absorbed. Fluff the grains with a fork.

2  Heat the olive oil in a large pan and stir fry the chorizo for 3–4 minutes. Remove with a slotted spoon and put aside. Add the onion to the oil left in the pan and cook for 5–6 minutes until softened.

3  Stir in the paprika, cook for 1 minute, then tip in the chickpeas and the chicken stock. Return the chorizo to the pan and simmer for 2 minutes. Spoon the chorizo mixture over the couscous and scatter with the chopped parsley.

• Per serving 424 kcalories, protein 18g, carbohydrate 46g, fat 20g, saturated fat 5g, fibre 3g, added sugar 0g, salt 1.69g

Polenta is a classic Italian ingredient, but you could try small chunks of unpeeled potato instead.

# Italian Chicken and Polenta

500g pack ready-to-use polenta
25g/1oz Parmesan, grated
2 skin-on boneless chicken breast fillets
250g pack cherry tomatoes
leaves from a few fresh rosemary sprigs, torn
1 garlic clove, sliced
2 tbsp olive oil
green salad, to serve

Takes 30 minutes • Serves 2

1  Pre-heat the oven to 220°C/Gas 7/fan 200°C. Using your fingers, roughly break up the polenta into small chunks and scatter over the bottom of a small roasting tin. Tip in the Parmesan and mix.
2  Sit the chicken breasts, cherry tomatoes, rosemary and garlic on top of the polenta, drizzle with olive oil, then season to taste.
3  Roast for 25 minutes until the chicken skin is crisp and golden and the polenta and cheese are turning crusty around the edges. Serve with a green salad.

• Per serving 513 kcalories, protein 40g, carbohydrate 47g, fat 20g, saturated fat 5g, fibre 7g, added sugar 0g, salt 4.63g

The perfect dish for those evenings when it's too late to shop on the
way home from work. Serve with a green salad and
a glass of red wine.

# Storecupboard Spaghetti Puttanesca

400g/14oz spaghetti
1 tbsp olive oil
1 onion, peeled and sliced
1 garlic clove, peeled and crushed
2 tbsp capers
400g can chopped tomatoes
pinch of paprika
100g/4oz roasted peppers, frozen or
from a jar, chopped
16 black olives, pitted
freshly grated Parmesan, to serve
(optional)

Takes 15 minutes • Serves 4

1  Cook the pasta according to the packet
instructions. Meanwhile, heat the oil in a large
frying pan and fry the onion over a medium
heat for 5 minutes until soft. Add the garlic
and cook for another minute.
2  Rinse the capers and add to the pan with
the tomatoes, paprika, peppers and olives.
Check for seasoning then cook for a few
minutes more until heated through.
3  Drain the pasta and toss with the
sauce. Serve with lots of grated Parmesan,
if you like.

• Per serving 433 kcalories, protein 14g, carbohydrate
82g, fat 8g, saturated fat 1g, fibre 6g, sugar 9g,
salt 1.38g

Treat this omelette like a pizza and add your favourite toppings to the egg base. Grilled peppers, sliced salami or sliced mushrooms all work well.

# Pizza Omelette

8 eggs
1 tsp dried oregano
1 tbsp olive oil
4 tbsp tomato pasta sauce (from a jar)
85g/3oz Cheddar, grated
handful of black olives, pitted
green salad, to serve

Takes 15 minutes • Serves 4

1 Heat the grill to high. Beat the eggs with the oregano and some salt and pepper.
2 Heat the oil in a large, ovenproof frying pan, then tip in the eggs. Cook over a low-ish heat for 4 minutes, stirring occasionally until the eggs are practically set. Place under the grill until set and puffed up.
3 Spread the sauce over the omelette, scatter with cheese and olives, then grill again until the cheese is melted. Cut into wedges and serve with a green salad.

• Per serving 318 kcalories, protein 21g, carbohydrate 1g, fat 26g, saturated fat 9g, fibre 1g, sugar 1g, salt 0.97g

Harissa is a red pepper paste that is commonly used in Moroccan cooking. It contains chillies, so it adds some real spice to this recipe.

# Hot Harissa Lamb with Couscous

4 tbsp harissa paste
300g/10oz couscous
120g bag herb salad
4 lamb leg steaks (about 600g/1lb 5oz in total)
2 tbsp demerara sugar

Takes 10 minutes, plus resting
Serves 4

1  Spoon one tablespoon of the harissa into a jug, fill with 400ml/14 fl oz of boiling water, then pour over the couscous in a large serving bowl. Cover and stand for 5 minutes. Fluff with a fork then empty the salad on top.
2  Heat a frying pan. Season the lamb, then fry for 1 minute each side. Mix the sugar and remaining harissa together and spread it over the lamb. Cook for 2 more minutes on each side, remove from pan and rest for 5 minutes.
3  Add a splash of water to the pan and boil the juices to make a sauce. Slice the lamb and serve on top of the salad with the sauce drizzled over.

• Per serving 505 kcalories, protein 34g, carbohydrate 48g, fat 21g, saturated fat 10g, fibre 0g, sugar 10g, salt 0.48g

All the classic ingredients in one dish make this a real taste of Italy, and so simple to prepare.

# Fresh Lasagne with Pesto

1.2 litres/2 pints milk
100g/4oz butter, cut into pieces
100g/4oz plain flour
pinch of freshly grated nutmeg
500g/1lb 2oz baby spinach leaves
250g/9oz fresh lasagne sheets
3 rounded tbsp good-quality pesto
500g/1lb 2oz cherry tomatoes on the vine, two or three vines left whole
good handful of basil leaves (or one supermarket pack)
175g/6oz fresh Parmesan, coarsely grated
2 x 125–150g balls mozzarella, preferably buffalo, torn into bite-sized pieces

Takes about 1¾ hours • Serves 6

1  Pre-heat the oven to 200°C/Gas 6/fan 180°C. Whisk milk, butter and flour in a pan until thickened. Simmer for 1 minute. Remove from the heat, season, and add the nutmeg. Cool. Put the spinach in a large heatproof bowl, pour over boiling water and leave for 30 seconds. Drain into a colander, cool under cold water then squeeze well.
2  Spread 1–2 tablespoons of sauce over the base of a 20 x 30 x 6cm/8 x 12 x 2½in ovenproof dish. Top with a third of the lasagne sheets. Spread over a third of sauce. Swirl a spoonful of pesto into the sauce. Scatter over half the spinach, a third of the tomatoes, some basil and a third of the cheeses. Repeat the layering until all the ingredients have been used. Bake for 35–40 minutes until golden.

• Per serving 711 kcalories, protein 38g, carbohydrate 46g, fat 43g, saturated fat 25g, fibre 4g, added sugar 0g, salt 2.5g

A traditional Spanish dish that's well worth the time it takes to cook.
Serve with chunky bread and a crisp green salad.

# Spanish Omelette

150ml/¼ pint extra virgin olive oil
500g/1lb 2oz new potatoes, cut into thick slices
1 onion, preferably white, peeled and chopped
6 eggs
3 tbsp chopped fresh flatleaf parsley

Takes about 1 hour • Serves 4

1  Heat the oil in a large frying pan, add the potatoes and onion and stew gently, partially covered, for 30 minutes, stirring occasionally until the potatoes are softened. Strain the potatoes and onions through a colander into a large bowl (set the strained oil aside).
2  Beat the eggs and stir into the potatoes with the parsley and plenty of salt and pepper. Heat a little of the strained oil in a smaller pan. Tip everything into the pan and cook on a moderate heat, using a spatula to shape the omelette into a cushion.
3  When almost set, invert on a plate and slide back into the pan and cook for a few more minutes. Invert twice more, cooking the omelette briefly each time and pressing the edges to keep the cushion shape. Slide on to a plate and cool for 10 minutes before serving.

• Per serving 516 kcalories, protein 12g, carbohydrate 23g, fat 43g, saturated fat 7g, fibre 2g, added sugar 0g, salt 0.31g

An impressive but simple pasta dish that will make you wonder why you ever bought pesto in a jar.

# Sicilian-style Pesto Pasta

300g/10oz linguine
85g/3oz whole blanched almonds, roughly chopped
25g/1oz caciocavallo or pecorino cheese, grated
large handful of basil leaves, roughly chopped
50ml/2fl oz extra virgin olive oil
4 small vine tomatoes, seeded and chopped

Takes 20 minutes • Serves 4

1  Cook the pasta according to the packet instructions. To make the pesto, blend together the almonds, cheese, most of the basil and all of the olive oil in a food processor until they form a chunky paste.
2  Drain the pasta and stir through the pesto and tomatoes.
3  Spoon on to serving plates and sprinkle with the remaining basil leaves.

• Per serving 528 kcalories, protein 16g, carbohydrate 60g, fat 27g, saturated fat 4g, fibre 4g, added sugar 0g, salt 0.16g

A super-fast, spicy supper or snack that's on the table in minutes.

# Spicy Sausage and Goats' Cheese Toasts

2 tbsp olive oil
1 fat red chilli, seeded and finely chopped
2 rolls, split (ciabatta works well), or 4 thick slices of bread
70g pack sliced chorizo or other spicy cured sausage
50g bag rocket
100g/4oz goats' cheese, crumbled

Takes 10 minutes • Serves 4 as a snack or 2 as a main meal

1 First mix the olive oil and chilli in a bowl.
2 While the flavours mingle, toast the split rolls or bread.
3 Top the bread with the sausage, rocket and goats' cheese, then drizzle over the chilli oil.

• Per serving 485 kcalories, protein 22g, carbohydrate 25g, fat 34g, saturated fat 14g, fibre 2g, added sugar 0g, salt 2.2g

Tabbouleh can be served as a salad on its own, but is also great alongside fish and chicken.

# Tabbouleh with Salmon

250g/9oz couscous
300ml/½ pint boiling vegetable stock
4 vine-ripened tomatoes
½ cucumber
1 bunch spring onions
2 x 20g packs fresh parsley
finely grated zest 1 lemon
6 tbsp olive oil
2 tbsp fresh lemon juice
1 garlic clove, crushed
4 grilled salmon fillets, to serve

Takes 15–20 minutes • Serves 4

1 Put the couscous into a large bowl, pour over the boiling stock and stir. Cover with a plate or cling film and leave to stand for 5 minutes or until all the liquid has been absorbed. Separate the grains by fluffing with a fork.

2 Finely dice the tomatoes and the cucumber. Slice the spring onions and finely chop the parsley, then add them to the couscous with the lemon zest.

3 Whisk the olive oil, lemon juice and garlic with plenty of seasoning and drizzle over the couscous. Toss well and serve with the grilled salmon.

• Per serving with salmon 591 kcalories, protein 35.9g, carbohydrate 37.5g, fat 34.1g, saturated fat 5.8g, fibre 2.4g, sugar 5.8g, salt 0.30g

A hearty one-pot dish that is delicious all year round.
A real family favourite.

# Turkish Lamb Pilau

small handful of pine nuts or flaked almonds
1 tbsp olive oil
1 large onion, halved, peeled and sliced
2 cinnamon sticks, broken in half
500g/1lb 2oz lean lamb neck fillet, cubed
250g/9oz basmati rice
1 lamb or vegetable stock cube
12 ready-to-eat dried apricots
handful of fresh mint leaves, roughly chopped

Takes 25–30 minutes • Serves 4

1  Dry fry the pine nuts or almonds in a large pan until lightly toasted, then tip on to a plate. Add the oil to the pan then fry the onion and cinnamon together until starting to turn golden.

2  Turn up the heat, stir in the lamb and fry until the meat changes colour. Tip in the rice and cook for 1 minute, stirring all the time.

3  Pour in 500ml/18fl oz boiling water, crumble in the stock cube, add the apricots and season to taste. Turn the heat down, cover and simmer for 12 minutes until the rice is tender and the stock has been absorbed. Toss in the pine nuts or almonds and mint and serve.

• Per serving 584 kcalories, protein 32g, carbohydrate 65g, fat 24g, saturated fat 9g, fibre 3g, added sugar 0g, salt 1.4g

From hob to table in just 20 minutes, it's ideal for
weeknight entertaining.

# Creamy Prawn Pasta

400g/14oz linguine
400g bag cooked frozen prawns,
thawed
100g bag rocket
3 tbsp crème fraîche
25g/1oz Parmesan, grated

Takes 20 minutes, plus thawing
Serves 4

1 Bring a large pan of water to the boil, then cook the linguine according to the packet instructions. Spoon out a little of the pasta cooking water and reserve, then tip in the prawns, just to heat through before draining.
2 Return the prawns and pasta to the pan then tip in the rest of the ingredients.
3 Toss everything together, adding enough of the reserved cooking water to moisten the pasta if it is dry. Serve straight away.

• Per serving 472 kcalories, protein 27g, carbohydrate 78g, fat 9g, saturated fat 4g, fibre 4g, sugar 3g, salt 1.05g

This is a great meat-free main dish – all it needs is a salad to go with it, or it can be served as an accompaniment to roast pork or lamb.

# Fennel and Tomato Gratin

**FOR THE FENNEL**
3 tbsp olive oil
4 fennel bulbs, trimmed (fronds kept) and cut into thin wedges
2 garlic cloves, peeled and chopped
400g can chopped tomatoes

**FOR THE TOPPING**
85g/3oz white bread, torn in pieces
50g/2oz Parmesan, grated
handful of fennel fronds
finely grated zest 1 lemon
handful of black olives, pitted

Takes 1 hour 10 minutes • Serves 4

1  Heat two tablespoons of the olive oil in a pan, then add the fennel, cover and stew over a low heat for 15 minutes. Add the garlic and continue to cook for 10–20 minutes until the fennel is soft (the timing depends on how thick it is). Add the tomatoes and simmer, uncovered, for 10 minutes until the fennel is coated in a thick tomato sauce. Tip everything into a shallow gratin dish. Pre-heat the oven to 200°C/Gas 6/fan 180°C.
2  While the fennel is cooking, tip all the topping ingredients, except the olives, into a food processor and blitz to crumbs. Add the olives and pulse until chopped, but not blended.
3  Scatter the crumbs generously over the fennel mixture, drizzle with the rest of the oil, then bake for 20 minutes until golden.

• Per serving 220 kcalories, protein 9g, carbohydrate 16g, fat 14g, saturated fat 4g, fibre 5g, sugar 5g, salt 0.86g

These stuffed tomatoes give a real taste of the Mediterranean on a summer's day.

# Couscous-stuffed Beef Tomatoes

150g/5oz couscous
4 beef tomatoes
1 garlic clove, peeled and crushed
1 tsp smoked paprika
4 spring onions, roughly sliced
1 bunch fresh coriander, roughly chopped
1 bunch fresh mint, roughly chopped
juice of 1 lemon
50g/2oz toasted pine nuts
50g/2oz sultanas
2 tbsp olive

Takes 40 minutes • Serves 4

1 Pre-heat the oven to 200°C/Gas 6/fan 180°C. Put the couscous in a heatproof bowl, pour over 175ml/6fl oz boiling water, cover and leave for 5 minutes. Cut across a third of the way down each tomato, discard the core and scoop out the inside keeping the outside of the tomato intact. Place the tomato bits in a bowl. Add the garlic, paprika and couscous. Leave for 1 minute before mixing with a fork.

2 Mix the spring onions, coriander, mint, lemon juice, pine nuts, sultanas, olive oil and seasoning. Add to the couscous and stir until combined.

3 Using a spoon, fill the tomato cases with the couscous mix. Top with the lids, place in a roasting tray, drizzle with a little olive oil and bake for 20 minutes until soft.

• Per serving 285 kcalories, protein 6g, carbohydrate 34g, fat 15g, saturated fat 2g, fibre 2g, sugar 14g, salt 0.04g

These are best served hot or at room temperature alongside a simple rocket salad for an easy lunch or supper.

# Pepper Pizzas

olive oil, for greasing and drizzling
4 peppers (2 red, 2 yellow), halved lengthways, seeded and cored
90g pack prosciutto
handful of fresh marjoram sprigs
2 garlic cloves, peeled and thinly sliced
4 plum tomatoes, halved lengthways
8 anchovies, halved lengthways
125–150g pack mozzarella, sliced

TO SERVE
handful of basil and rocket leaves
Parmesan shavings
8 black olives, unpitted
ciabatta or focaccia

Takes 55 minutes • Serves 4

1 Pre-heat the oven to 200°C/Gas 6/fan 180°C. Lightly oil an ovenproof dish or roasting tin and put the peppers in. If wobbly, trim a small slice off the bottom. Insert a prosciutto slice into each pepper, so it hangs over the edge slightly. Scatter on the marjoram and garlic then sit a tomato half on top. Drape over the anchovies. Drizzle with olive oil, season and roast for 35 minutes or until the peppers are soft.
2 Halve the mozzarella slices and lay 2 halves on each pepper. Put back in the oven for a few minutes to melt the cheese.
3 Scatter each pepper with basil, rocket and Parmesan, add an olive, drizzle on oil and add pepper. Serve with ciabatta or focaccia.

• Per portion 242 kcalories, protein 16.4g, carbohydrate 12.2g, fat 14.6g, saturated fat 6.1g, fibre 3.7g, sugar 11.4g, salt 1.77g

A quick variation on a traditional Moroccan dish, this easy recipe is perfect for a comforting veggie supper.

# Vegetable Tagine with Chickpea Couscous

400g pack shallots, peeled and cut in half
2 tbsp olive oil
1 large butternut squash, about 1.25kg/2 lb 12oz, peeled, seeded and cut into bite-sized chunks
1 tsp ground cinnamon
½ tsp ground ginger
450ml/16 fl oz strong-flavoured vegetable stock
12 small pitted prunes
2 tsp clear honey
2 red peppers, seeded and cut into chunks
3 tbsp chopped fresh coriander
2 tbsp chopped fresh mint, plus extra for sprinkling

FOR THE COUSCOUS
250g/9oz couscous
1 tbsp harissa paste
400g can chickpeas, drained and rinsed
handful of toasted flaked almonds

Takes 35 minutes • Serves 4

1  Fry the shallots in the oil for 5 minutes until they are softening and browned. Add the squash and spices and stir for 1 minute. Pour in the stock, season well, then add the prunes and honey. Cover and simmer for 8 minutes.

2  Add the peppers and cook for 8–10 minutes until just tender. Stir in the coriander and mint.

3  Pour 400ml/14fl oz boiling water over the couscous in a bowl, then stir in the harissa with half a teaspoon of salt. Tip in the chickpeas, then cover and leave for 5 minutes. Fluff up with a fork and serve with the tagine, flaked almonds and extra mint.

• Per serving 483 kcalories, protein 15g, carbohydrate 85g, fat 11g, saturated fat 1g, fibre 10g, sugar 33g, salt 0.61g

For an extra Mediterranean flavour, add one tablespoon of capers, a handful of pitted black olives and a few chopped anchovies.

# Ratatouille

4 large ripe tomatoes, skins removed
5 tbsp olive oil
2 large aubergines, cut into
1.5cm/⅝in chunks
4 small courgettes, cut into
1.5cm/⅝in slices
2 red or yellow peppers, seeded,
cut into bite-sized chunks
1 medium onion, peeled and thinly
sliced
3 garlic cloves, peeled and crushed
1 tbsp red wine vinegar
1 tsp sugar (any kind)
supermarket pack or small bunch
basil, leaves torn

Takes 50 minutes • Serves 4

1  Quarter the tomatoes, scrape away the seeds with a spoon, and chop the flesh.
2  Heat a frying pan over a medium heat, then pour in two tablespoons of the olive oil. Brown the aubergines for 5 minutes on each side until soft. Set them aside and fry the courgettes in another tablespoon of oil for 5 minutes, until golden on both sides. Repeat with the peppers. Don't overcook the vegetables at this stage, as they have more cooking to do in the next step.
3  Cook the onion in the pan in the remaining oil for 5 minutes. Add the garlic and fry for another minute. Stir in the vinegar and sugar, then tip in the tomatoes and half the basil. Return the vegetables to the pan with some salt and pepper and cook for 5 minutes. Serve with the remaining basil.

• Per serving 241 kcalories, protein 6g, carbohydrate 20g, fat 16g, saturated fat 2g, fibre 8g, sugar 18g, salt 0.05g

A delicately flavoured alternative to traditional roast potatoes, these wedges are ideal for serving with chicken, lamb or fish.

# Lemon and Rosemary Potato Wedges

1kg/2lb 4oz large-ish waxy potatoes
3 tbsp olive oil
juice 2 lemons
1 tbsp chopped fresh rosemary or 1 tsp dried
6–8 garlic cloves, kept whole in skins

Takes 40–50 minutes • Serves 4

1  Pre-heat the oven to 200°C/Gas 6/fan 180°C. Peel the potatoes and cut into thick wedges. Put in a pan, pour in enough water to cover and bring to the boil. Simmer for 2 minutes, then drain well, shaking the colander.
2  Put the olive oil, lemon juice, rosemary and garlic in a roasting tin with some salt and pepper. Add the potatoes and toss well until they are coated and glistening. Leave for 10 minutes to soak up the oil and lemon.
3  Bake for 20–30 minutes, shaking the tin halfway through, until the potatoes are nicely browned and glossy.

• Per serving 227 kcalories, protein 4g, carbohydrate 35g, fat 9g, saturated fat 1g, fibre 3g, sugar 2g, salt 0.29g

Cavolo nero, a dark green Italian cabbage, is often served as a side dish or tossed through pasta, but it can also be used as an excellent addition to a stir fry.

# Cavolo Nero with Garlic and Bacon

1kg/2lb 4oz cavolo nero
25g/1oz butter
8 rashers rindless smoked bacon, cut into chunks
2 garlic cloves, peeled and sliced in slivers

Takes 25 minutes • Serves 4

1  To prepare the cavolo nero: hold the stalks in one hand and use the other hand to strip the leaves from them. Discard the stalks and roughly chop the leaves.

2  Bring a large pan of water to the boil, add the cavolo nero and blanch for 1 minute until wilted. Drain.

3  Heat the butter in a frying pan and fry the bacon for 6–8 minutes until starting to crisp. Throw in the garlic and sizzle for a moment. Add the cavolo nero, cover and cook for 5 minutes until soft. Season with salt and pepper and serve immediately.

• Per serving 155 kcalories, protein 10g, carbohydrate 5g, fat 11g, saturated fat 5g, fibre 1g, added sugar none, salt 2.58g

A delicious and super-healthy dish that makes a light supper or the perfect accompaniment to seasonal spring lamb.

# Broad Beans with Tomatoes and Anchovies

1.3kg/3lb young broad beans in the pod (about 350g/12oz shelled beans)
3 tbsp olive oil
450g/1lb cherry tomatoes, halved
6 spring onions, finely chopped
2 garlic cloves, peeled and sliced
4–6 anchovy fillets, chopped
2 tbsp chopped fresh marjoram or parsley

Takes 20–25 minutes • Serves 4

1 Blanch the shelled beans in boiling water for 1 minute. Drain into a sieve and hold under running cold water to cool them down quickly. Drain again and peel off the outer hard skins – make a nick in the tops and pop the beans out.

2 Heat the oil in a non-stick frying pan until very hot, add the tomatoes and sauté over a high heat until the juices begin to run and caramelize. Tip in the spring onions and garlic and cook over a medium heat for 1–2 minutes until the onions just begin to soften and the garlic begins to turn golden.

3 Add the beans and sauté for 1–2 minutes until heated through. Stir in the anchovies so they break up, season to taste with salt and freshly ground black pepper, then stir in the marjoram or parsley and serve.

• Per serving 161 kcalories, protein 7g, carbohydrate 11g, fat 10g, saturated fat 1g, fibre 7g, added sugar 0g, salt 0.34g

This salad is full of big Mediterranean flavours and a little sherry vinegar adds a touch of authenticity to the dressing.

# Spanish Chicken and Chickpea Salad

2 x 410g cans chickpeas, drained and rinsed
300g pack vine-ripened cherry tomatoes, halved
290g jar marinated peppers in oil, halved
1 medium roasted chicken
small bunch flatleaf parsley, roughly chopped, to garnish

FOR THE DRESSING
2 garlic cloves, peeled and crushed
2 tbsp sherry vinegar
6 tbsp oil from the pepper jar
½ tsp smoked paprika
juice ½ an orange

Takes 20 minutes • Serves 6

1  First, make the dressing. Using a stick blender or mini processor, whiz together the garlic, vinegar, pepper oil, smoked paprika and orange juice until smooth. If you don't have a blender, simply crush the garlic and whisk together with all of the other ingredients.
2  In a large bowl, mix together the chickpeas, cherry tomatoes and the peppers. Pour over half of the dressing, season and spoon on to a large serving platter.
3  Place the chicken on a board and pull the flesh from the bones. Cut or tear the chicken into bite-sized pieces, then pile on top of the salad. Drizzle over the remaining dressing, scatter with the parsley and serve.

• Per serving 505 kcalories, protein 31g, carbohydrate 18g, fat 35g, saturated fat 7g, fibre 5g, sugar 5g, salt 1.31g

You need firm bread with good structure for this salad, as a softer loaf will disintegrate. If you don't have ciabatta, use any country loaf with a good crust or some pitta bread.

# Tuna and Caper Panzanella

3 slices ciabatta, preferably a day or two old
4–5 tomatoes
½ cucumber
8–10 basil leaves
200g can tuna
2 tsp capers, drained and roughly chopped
2 tbsp red wine vinegar
4 tbsp olive oil

Takes 15 minutes • Serves 2

1  Dip the bread briefly into cold water, then squeeze well and crumble into a bowl. Halve the tomatoes and squeeze out the seeds, then roughly chop the flesh. Chop the cucumber into small chunks.
2  Add the tomato and cucumber to the bread, then tear in the basil leaves.
3  Drain and flake the tuna into chunks, add to the bread with the capers, vinegar, oil and salt and pepper to taste. Mix everything well and serve.

• Per serving 463 kcalories, protein 27g, carbohydrate 21g, fat 31g, saturated fat 5g, fibre 3g, sugar 6g, salt 1.35g

The ready-to-eat chorizo is better for this salad than the cooking variety: it's similar in size to salami and you can buy it thinly sliced to order from the deli counter or in packs.

# Garlicky Bean Salad with Chorizo

400g can cannellini or other white beans
1 small red onion, peeled and thinly sliced
2 tbsp red wine vinegar
140g/5oz button mushrooms, thinly sliced
handful of flatleaf parsley, coarsely chopped
3 tbsp olive oil
100g/4oz thinly sliced chorizo
crusty bread, to serve

Takes 15 minutes • Serves 2

1  Rinse and drain the beans, then pat dry with kitchen paper. Mix the onion with the vinegar and leave for 5 minutes to soak.
2  Mix the mushrooms and parsley into the beans. Add the onions and vinegar, oil and seasoning and mix well.
3  Arrange overlapping slices of chorizo over two plates and spoon the salad in the centre. Serve with crusty bread.

• Per serving 449 kcalories, protein 21g, carbohydrate 27g, fat 30g, saturated fat 7g, fibre 8g, sugar 6g, salt 2.05g

Use a fruity Sicilian olive oil, or similar, to bring out the classic
Mediterranean flavours of this fresh and zingy salad.

# Tomato and Mint Salad

400g/14oz cherry tomatoes,
1 small red onion, peeled
handful of fresh mint leaves
extra virgin olive oil, to drizzle
finely grated zest 1 lemon, to garnish

Takes 10 minutes • Serves 6

1  Halve the cherry tomatoes and scatter
over a large plate. Finely chop the red onion
and tear up the mint leaves.
2  Throw the onion and mint over the
tomatoes. This can be made 3–4 hours
ahead and kept covered.
3  Just before serving, drizzle with extra virgin
olive oil, season with salt and ground black
pepper and finely grate a little lemon zest over
the top.

• Per serving 62 kcalories, protein 1g, carbohydrate
3g, fat 5g, saturated fat 1g, fibre 1g, added sugar
none, salt 0.02g

This vibrant dish makes a zesty salad course or a light and sophisticated starter.

# Halloumi Salad with Orange and Mint

3 medium oranges, segments and juice
1 small bunch fresh mint, leaves chopped
4 tsp white wine vinegar
3 tbsp olive oil
2 x 250g packs halloumi cheese, drained
50g/2oz walnut pieces, toasted
145g bag rocket, watercress and spinach

Takes 20 minutes • Serves 4

1  Heat a large griddle or frying pan over a high heat. In a large bowl, combine the orange segments and juice, mint leaves, vinegar and olive oil. Season and gently toss together.

2  Slice each block of halloumi into 8–10 pieces, then griddle or fry for 1–2 minutes on each side until charred and beginning to melt.

3  Add the walnuts and salad leaves to the orange and mint. Toss together. Top with the griddled halloumi slices and season with some black pepper.

• Per serving 581 kcalories, protein 28g, carbohydrate 12g, fat 47g, saturated fat 20g, fibre 3g, sugar 12g, salt 4.41g

The mint and lemon really give this salad a fresh, lively flavour; it's perfect as a light lunch or as an accompaniment to a summer barbecue.

# Aubergine, Lemon and Pepper Salad

2 aubergines, diced
1 red onion, peeled and chopped
6 garlic cloves, kept whole
2 red peppers, seeded and chopped
4 tbsp olive oil
4 vine tomatoes, chopped
finely grated zest and juice 1 lemon
4 tbsp chopped fresh mint
100g/4oz black olives, pitted

Takes 45 minutes • Serves 6

1  Pre-heat the oven to 220°C/Gas 7/fan 200°C. Toss the aubergines, onion, garlic and peppers together with the oil, then roast for 30 minutes until the vegetables are tender. Tip into a bowl. This can be done a day ahead.

2  Add the tomatoes, lemon zest and juice, then season.

3  Stir in the mint and olives. This will keep in the fridge for a few hours, but bring to room temperature before serving.

• Per serving 145 kcalories, protein 3g, carbohydrate 10g, fat 11g, saturated fat 1g, fibre 4g, sugar 8g, salt 0.28g

A fabulously quick and colourful dish that tastes great whether eaten hot or cold.

# Spiced Herb and Almond Couscous

2 tbsp olive oil
2 red onions, halved, peeled and sliced
pinch of saffron strands (optional)
425ml/¾ pint hot chicken stock (from a cube is fine)
1 fat red chilli, sliced
500g/1lb 2oz couscous
2 x 20g packs fresh coriander, leaves only
50g/2oz whole toasted almonds
handful of dates, roughly chopped (Medjool dates are good)
juice ½ lemon

Takes 10 minutes, plus 10 minutes standing • Serves 6

1  Heat the oil in a roasting tin, add the onions and fry for about 5 minutes until just softened. While you're frying, add the saffron strands (if using) to the stock, so the flavour and colour infuses.
2  Tip the chilli into the tin, fry for 1 minute more, then take off the heat. Add the couscous and stock, then cover with cling film for 10 minutes.
3  Once the couscous has absorbed all the stock, quickly chop the coriander (if you chop it too soon it will start to wilt), then fork it through the couscous with the almonds, dates and lemon juice and serve straight away. To serve cold, leave to cool, then add the chopped coriander just before eating.

• Per serving 297 kcalories, protein 10g, carbohydrate 53g, fat 6g, saturated fat 1g, fibre 2g, sugar 10g, salt 0.37g

A fresh, light lunch or side salad that encompasses all the flavours of a Mediterranean summer.

# Greek Salad

1 medium red onion
1 tsp dried oregano
2 tbsp white wine vinegar
8 tbsp Greek extra virgin olive oil
4 ripe medium-sized tomatoes
1 cucumber
2 handfuls of Kalamata black olives, pitted
2 fresh oregano sprigs, finely chopped
200g pack feta

Takes 20–25 minutes, plus marinating
Serves 4

1  Halve, peel and slice the onion, tip the slices into a bowl and sprinkle over the dried oregano. Pour in the vinegar and olive oil, stir well, cover and set aside for a couple of hours.
2  Cut the tomatoes into chunks. Quarter the cucumber lengthways and slice thickly across. Tip the tomatoes and cucumber into a salad bowl and add the onion, olives and half the fresh oregano. Season, if you wish.
3  Crumble the feta roughly over the top of the salad and sprinkle with the remaining oregano. Stir together, taking care not to break up the feta.

• Per serving 369 kcalories, protein 10g, carbohydrate 7g, fat 34g, saturated fat 10g, fibre 2g, added sugar none, salt 2.58g

A classic dish made simple – the ideal meal for a lazy summer's lunch or outdoors supper.

# Salade Niçoise

5 tbsp olive oil, plus a little extra for frying and drizzling
2 tsp finely chopped fresh oregano
1½–2 tbsp fresh lemon juice
16 new potatoes, halved
100g/4oz green beans
4x100g/4oz fresh tuna steaks
handful of black olives, pitted
8 anchovy fillets, thinly sliced in strips
16 cherry tomatoes, halved
4 small eggs, soft-boiled, halved
grated Parmesan, to serve

Takes about 35 minutes • Serves 4

1  Whisk the five tablespoons of olive oil with the oregano and enough of the lemon juice to taste, in a large bowl. Season, set aside.
2  Cook the potatoes in boiling, salted water for 10 minutes, or until tender, adding the beans for the last 4 minutes. Drain well and toss while warm in the dressing.
3  Heat a little oil in a large frying pan, add the tuna and fry over a high heat for 2–3 minutes on each side. Add the olives, anchovies and tomatoes to the potatoes and gently toss. Scatter the salad over four plates, top with the tuna, eggs, Parmesan and a drizzle of oil.

• Per portion 523 kcalories, protein 34.8g, carbohydrate 24.9g, fat 32.3g, saturated fat 5.6g, fibre 2.8g, sugar 3.9g, salt 1.08g

This is great served with grilled meat or chicken and also makes a simple lunch for vegetarians with some toasted or griddled pitta breads.

# Smoked Aubergine Purée

2 medium aubergines
juice 1 lemon
2–3 garlic cloves, peeled and crushed
150ml carton thick natural yoghurt
small bunch fresh dill, leaves chopped

Takes 35 minutes • Serves 4

1  Pre-heat the grill to very hot. Slice the aubergines in half lengthways, then grill for 25 minutes, turning occasionally, until soft – the skin will remain firm, but the flesh will soften. Lift the aubergines off the grill and leave until cool enough to handle.
2  Using a sharp knife, score the grilled flesh and scoop out the flesh with a spoon.
Tip it into a bowl and mash with a fork until you get a thick pulp. Beat in the lemon juice and garlic.
3  Mix in the yoghurt and dill, and season. Serve while still warm.

• Per serving 77 kcalories, protein 4g, carbohydrate 6g, fat 5g, saturated fat 2g, fibre 3g, sugar 5g, salt 0.07g

A favourite dip for all ages, any time of year, and the ideal snack or lunch.

# Home-made Houmous with Baked Pitta Crisps

6 mini pitta breads, split in half then cut into two
2 tbsp olive oil
¼ tsp sea salt

FOR THE HOUMOUS
410g can chickpeas, drained and rinsed
juice 2 lemons
2 garlic cloves, peeled and crushed
2 tbsp olive oil
¼ tsp sea salt
150ml/¼pt tahini paste (optional)

Takes 20 minutes • Serves 4, or 6–8 as a snack

1  Pre-heat the oven to 200°C/Gas 6/fan 180°C. Spread the pitta pieces over a large roasting tin. Drizzle with the olive oil and sprinkle with sea salt. Bake for 6 minutes or until they are just beginning to brown and become crispy. Serve warm or cold. They will keep in an airtight container for up to 4 days.
2  To make the houmous, whiz the chickpeas, lemon juice, garlic, olive oil, sea salt and tahini paste (if using) in a food processor until just smooth. Loosen with a little water if needed. Tip into a bowl and serve with the pitta crisps. The houmous will keep in the fridge for up to 3 days.

• Per serving (if serving 4) 307 kcalories, protein 10g, carbohydrate 40g, fat 14g, saturated fat 2g, fibre 4g, sugar 2g, salt 1.24g

A classic Spanish sauce, delicious with roasted vegetables or fish.

# Roasted Vegetables with Romesco Sauce

**FOR THE ROASTED VEGETABLES**
3 yellow and 3 red peppers,
seeded, each cut into 4 pieces
1 large fennel bulb, cut into 6 wedges
2 large onions, peeled, each cut
into 6 wedges
4 tbsp extra virgin olive oil
6 large spring onions

**FOR THE ROMESCO SAUCE**
6 tbsp olive oil
2 dried sweet peppers, such as
Nyora or choricero
1 dried chilli pepper
6–8 garlic cloves, peeled, kept whole
1 slice white bread, crusts removed,
bread broken in rough pieces
1 tbsp chopped fresh parsley
10 whole blanched almonds, toasted
12 hazelnuts, toasted
1 tomato, grilled and skin peeled
2 tbsp white wine vinegar

Takes 1½ hours • Serves 6

1  Pre-heat the oven to 220°C/Gas 7/fan 200°C. Put the peppers, fennel and onions in two roasting tins, toss with the oil. Roast for 45 minutes, adding the spring onions for the last 20 minutes. Season.

2  Make the sauce. Heat a tablespoon of the oil in a frying pan, fry the dried peppers and chilli until crisp. Remove, cool and break into pieces. Set aside. Fry four garlic cloves and the bread in the pan until golden. Remove, set aside. Crush remaining garlic, add fried garlic and peppers, crush. Add parsley, toasted nuts and bread. Pound to a fine paste.

3  Scoop out the tomato seeds. Mix the flesh with the paste. Add the olive oil and vinegar gradually, stirring constantly. Season. Peel off the pepper skins. Serve roasted vegetables warm on a platter with the sauce.

• Per portion 333 kcalories, protein 6.0g, carbohydrate 22g, fat 25.2g, saturated fat 3.1g, fibre 6.4g, sugar 14.4g, salt 0.11g

There's nothing better than the real thing with this classic sauce. Use to liven up pasta, chicken and summer veg.

# Pesto Sauce

100g/4oz pine nuts
100g/4oz Parmesan, cut into cubes
2 garlic cloves, quartered
20g pack fresh basil, leaves only
20g pack fresh flatleaf parsley, leaves only
100ml/3½ fl oz olive oil, plus extra for storing

Takes 10 minutes
Makes 300ml/½ pint

1 Put pine nuts, cheese, garlic, basil and parsley in a food processor and whiz until coarsely chopped.
2 With the machine running, slowly and steadily pour in the oil.
3 Taste and add seasoning if you like, but don't overdo it as the Parmesan is salty. Will keep in the fridge for up to a week. To keep it fresh, cover the surface with a thin layer of olive oil.

• Per 15ml portion 85 kcalories, protein 2.3g, carbohydrate 0.4g, fat 8.2g, saturated fat 1.7g, fibre 0.1g, sugar 0.2g, salt 0.08g

Perfect as a starter or as part of a buffet, aïoli gives a taste of summer all year round.

# Crudités with Herb Aïoli

100g/4oz French beans
4–6 spring onions, halved lengthways
2–3 Little Gem lettuces, cut into wedges
4 courgettes, cut into slim sticks
1 fennel bulb, cut into wedges (optional)

FOR THE HERB AÏOLI
1 plump garlic clove, crushed
½ tsp Dijon mustard
1 large egg yolk
150ml/¼ pint extra virgin olive oil (if very fruity, replace half with sunflower oil)
3–4 tbsp chopped fresh basil, mint or parsley
fresh lemon juice, to taste

Takes 20–25 minutes • Serves 6–8

1 Blanch the French beans in boiling salted water for 3–4 minutes. Refresh in cold water, drain and set aside.

2 For the aïoli, whisk together the garlic, mustard and a pinch of salt. Add the egg yolk and mix again. Next, add the oil a drop at a time, whisking continuously. Once the mixture begins to thicken, add the oil in a fine trickle, whisking vigorously all the time. If the aïoli is too thick, mix in about two to three teaspoons of warm water to get the right coating consistency for dipping vegetables in. Mix in the chopped herbs, taste, and adjust the flavour with a dash of lemon juice and salt if needed.

3 Spoon the aïoli into a bowl, cover and store in the fridge until needed. (This can be prepared a few hours ahead.) Arrange the vegetables on a platter and serve with the aïoli.

• Per serving for six 243 kcalories, protein 3g, carbohydrate 3g, fat 24g, saturated fat 4g, fibre 2g, added sugar none, salt 0.04g

Once you've made and tasted this simple soup you won't want to buy the tinned variety again.

# Tomato Soup with Gremolata

1 onion, peeled and chopped
2 garlic cloves, peeled and crushed
4 tbsp olive oil
2kg/4lb 8oz tomatoes
2 tbsp caster sugar
2 tbsp white wine vinegar

FOR THE GREMOLATA
finely grated zest and juice 1 lemon
3 tbsp olive oil
2 garlic cloves, peeled and crushed
bunch flatleaf parsley, finely chopped

Takes 1 hour 10 minutes • Serves 4

1 In a large shallow pan, fry the onion and garlic in the olive oil on a low heat for 8 minutes – do not brown. Roughly chop the tomatoes and add along with the sugar, vinegar, 750ml/1 pint 7fl oz water and some seasoning. Bring to the boil and simmer for 35 minutes, stirring from time to time.
2 Whiz with a hand-held blender until smooth. For an ultra-smooth, dinner-party-style soup, you can pass the liquid through a fine sieve, but this is quite fiddly.
3 For the gremolata, mix together the lemon zest, juice, olive oil, garlic and parsley, then serve on top of the soup.

• Per serving 307 kcalories, protein 4g, carbohydrate 27g, fat 21g, saturated fat 3g, fibre 6g, sugar 25g, salt 0.13g

To give this soup extra zing, stir in the zest of one lemon when you add the pesto.

# Summery Soup with Pesto

1 courgette, halved and thinly sliced
200g/8oz frozen peas, defrosted
1 vegetable or chicken stock cube
or concentrate
250g bag ready-cooked basmati rice
(or leftover cooked, cooled rice)
100g bag baby spinach
4 tbsp pesto (fresh from the chiller
cabinet or home made for the
best flavour and colour)
olive oil, for drizzling (optional)
grated Parmesan and crusty bread,
to serve

Takes 15 minutes, plus thawing
Serves 4

1 Boil the kettle. Tip the courgette and peas into a large bowl and cover with boiling water. Cover the bowl then leave for 3 minutes until the vegetables have softened slightly. Meanwhile, re-boil the kettle and make up 600ml/1 pint of stock and taste it for seasoning, as this is the base of the soup.
2 Drain the veg, then put back into the bowl along with the rice and spinach leaves. Pour over the hot stock, then cover and leave for another 2 minutes until heated through and the spinach has wilted.
3 Season to taste then ladle the soup into serving bowls. Add a swirl of pesto, olive oil, if using, and the grated Parmesan. Serve with crusty bread.

• Per serving 176 kcalories, protein 9g, carbohydrate 25g, fat 5g, saturated fat 2g, fibre 4g, added sugar none, salt 1.4g

A really warming, comforting and substantial soup that is also a quick and low-fat meal in itself.

# Chunky Mediterranean Fish Soup

500g tub Napoletana (tomato and basil) pasta sauce
450ml/12fl oz fish stock
2 courgettes, finely sliced
1 bulb fennel, finely sliced
450g/1lb white fish fillets
handful of basil leaves, torn

TO SERVE
1 tsp chipotle chillies in adobo sauce, or chilli paste
5 tbsp half-fat crème fraîche

Takes 15–20 minutes • Serves 4

1  Tip the pasta sauce and stock into a large pan, bring to the boil and simmer for 2–3 minutes. Add the courgettes and fennel and simmer for 2 minutes.
2  Cut the fish fillets into 4cm/1½ in pieces. Add to the soup and poach over a low heat for 2–3 minutes or until the fish is cooked. Don't stir too often or the fish will break up. Gently stir in the basil and adjust the seasoning.
3  Mix the chipotle chilli mix or chilli paste with the crème fraîche and season. Ladle the soup into bowls and spoon a dollop of the crème fraîche mixture on top.

• Per serving 164 kcalories, protein 23g, carbohydrate 9g, fat 4g, saturated fat 1g, fibre 3g, sugar 5g, salt 1.83g

While peaches are in season, this mouth-watering dish can be found on restaurant menus all over Italy.

# Prosciutto-wrapped Peaches

1 red chilli, seeded and finely chopped
8 tbsp olive oil
3 peaches, each cut into 4 wedges
2 x 125–150g balls mozzarella, torn into 12 chunks
12 slices prosciutto
handful of rocket leaves, to garnish

Takes 20 minutes • Serves 4

1 Mix the chilli with the olive oil and set aside.
2 Take a peach wedge and a mozzarella chunk, and wrap a slice of prosciutto around the two.
3 Place three peach parcels on each plate, scatter with a few rocket leaves and drizzle everything with the chilli oil just before serving.

• Per serving 483 kcalories, protein 24g, carbohydrate 7g, fat 40g, saturated fat 13g, fibre 1g, sugar 6g, salt 2.79g

A savoury ice may seem an unusual idea for a starter, but try it and you'll be surprised at how well it works.

# Tomato and Basil Granita

900g/2lb very ripe tomatoes
1 tsp salt
1 tbsp caster sugar
1 garlic clove, peeled and finely chopped
1 tsp ground black pepper
1 tbsp red wine vinegar
bunch basil, leaves removed from stalks

Takes 25 minutes, plus optional overnight macerating • Serves 8

1  Chop the tomatoes and place them in a bowl with all the other ingredients except the basil leaves. If you have time, leave them to macerate at room temperature overnight.

2  Place a metal tray with sides in the freezer to chill. Blitz everything in a blender – in batches – then strain through a fine sieve. Shred the basil leaves and stir through.

3  Pour the mix into the tray, cover with cling film and freeze until frozen around the edges and slushy in the middle. Use a fork to break the ice into smaller crystals. Return the tray to the freezer, repeat the breaking-up process every half hour (at least three times) until completely frozen and the texture of snow.

• Per serving 30 kcalories, protein 1g, carbohydrate 6g, fat none, saturated fat none, fibre 1g, sugar 6g, salt 0.65g

Sauce vierge is the Mediterranean version of a tomato salsa, which is used as a pasta sauce or salad dressing. Any that's left over will keep in the fridge for three days.

# Tomato Sauce Vierge with Scallops

### FOR THE SAUCE
100ml/4fl oz extra virgin olive oil
2 garlic cloves, peeled and very finely sliced
1 tsp coriander seeds
500g/1lb 2oz ripe tomatoes
3 tbsp red wine vinegar
small handful each of basil, coriander and parsley leaves, finely chopped

### FOR THE SCALLOPS
12 large scallops
drizzle of olive oil

Takes 35 minutes • Serves 4

1  For the sauce, warm the oil, garlic and coriander seeds very gently in a pan, then set aside. Nick a small cross in the bottom of each tomato, tip them into a large bowl and pour a kettleful of boiling water over them. Leave for about 10 seconds, drain and cool under cold water.

2  Peel and halve the tomatoes, squeeze out the seeds then roughly chop the flesh. Tip the tomato flesh into a bowl and season with salt and pepper. Stir in the vinegar, flavoured oil and herbs. Set aside for at least 20 minutes so all the flavours mingle.

3  For the scallops, heat a pan until very hot, toss the scallops with a drizzle of olive oil and sear for about 1 minute on each side until nicely caramelized. Spoon a pool of tomatoes on to plates and top each with three scallops.

• Per serving 387 kcalories, protein 30g, carbohydrate 5g, fat 28g, saturated fat 4g, fibre 1g, sugar 4g, salt 0.88g

This is a great little starter for entertaining as you can pre-cook and stuff the mussels several hours ahead of serving, then all that's needed is for it to be quickly flashed under the grill.

# Crunchy Baked Mussels

1kg/2lb 4oz mussels in their shells
50g/2oz toasted breadcrumbs
finely grated zest 1 lemon
100g/4oz garlic and parsley butter
(or mix 1 crushed garlic clove and
2 tbsp finely chopped fresh
parsley with 100g/4oz softened
butter)

Takes about 30 minutes • Serves 4

1  Scrub the mussels and pull off any beards. Rinse in several changes of cold water, then discard any that are open and do not close when tapped against the side of the sink.
2  Drain the mussels and put in a large pan with a splash of water. Bring to the boil, then cover the pan, shaking occasionally, until the mussels are open – this will take 2–3 minutes. Drain well and discard any that remain closed. Heat the grill to high.
3  Mix the crumbs and lemon zest. Remove one side of each shell and spread a little garlic butter on to each mussel. Set on a baking sheet and sprinkle with crumbs. Grill for 3–4 minutes until crunchy.

• Per serving 301 kcalories, protein 11g, carbohydrate 15g, fat 22g, saturated fat 13g, fibre 1g, sugar 1g, salt 1.06g

Grilling radicchio makes it taste slightly sweet and serving it with salty Parma ham and Parmesan creates a mouth-tingling combination.

# Radicchio Antipasti

2 heads radicchio
3 tbsp olive oil
aged balsamic vinegar, to drizzle
8 slices Serrano or Parma ham
100g/4oz Parmesan, shaved

Takes 10 minutes • Serves 4

1 Trim the outer leaves from the radicchio and cut it into wedges.
2 Heat a griddle pan over a medium heat, drizzle the radicchio with one tablespoon of oil and griddle for 1–2 minutes until wilted and lightly charred. Remove from the heat and drizzle with a little more oil and the balsamic vinegar.
3 Pile the leaves into the middle of four plates, drape the ham around and scatter over the Parmesan shavings.

• Per serving 238 kcalories, protein 16g, carbohydrate 3g, fat 18g, saturated fat 7g, fibre 1g, sugar 2g, salt 1.72g

An ideal make-ahead starter that can be served warm or cold
with a little salad.

# Pork Terrine with Prosciutto and Oregano

2 slices fresh white bread, crusts removed
500g/1lb 2oz pack minced pork
1 onion, peeled and roughly chopped
1 garlic clove, peeled and roughly chopped
big handful of fresh flatleaf parsley
1 tbsp chopped fresh oregano or 1 tsp dried
4 tbsp freshly grated Parmesan
1 egg, beaten
8 slices prosciutto

Takes 1 hour 20 minutes •
Cuts into 8–10 slices

1  Pre-heat the oven to 190°C/Gas 5/fan 170°C. Blitz the bread in a processor to make crumbs, then tip into a bowl with the pork. Add onion, garlic and herbs to the processor, process until finely chopped. Add to the bowl with the Parmesan and egg. Finely chop two slices of prosciutto. Add to the mix, combining well with salt and pepper.
2  Use the rest of the prosciutto to line a 1.5 litre/2¾ pint loaf tin. Spoon in the meat mix and press down. Flip the overhanging prosciutto over the top. Put the loaf tin into a roasting tin. Fill the roasting tin with water to halfway up the loaf tin. Bake for 1 hour until the 'loaf' shrinks from the sides of tin.
3  Remove from the oven and cool for 10 minutes. Drain off any excess liquid, turn out on to a board and slice. Serve warm or cold

• Per serving for eight 180 kcalories, protein 18g, carbohydrate 5g, fat 10g, saturated fat 4g, fibre 1g, sugar 1g, salt 0.63g

Serve these as a starter with finger bowls and a stack of paper napkins; break the shells by running your fingers along the inside, peel them off and eat.

# Langoustines with Tarragon

600g/1lb 5oz langoustine tails or raw headless prawns in shells
juice 1 lemon
2 tbsp olive oil
knob of butter
2 shallots, peeled and chopped
1 tbsp Cognac or brandy
2 tbsp chopped fresh tarragon
3 rounded tbsp crème fraîche
crusty baguettes, to serve

Takes 20–25 minutes • Serves 6

1  Wash the langoustines or prawns and pat dry. Toss them in the lemon juice in a bowl. Heat the oil in a pan, add the langoustines and fry, stirring all the time, for 5 minutes. Add the butter and chopped shallots and cook for a further 2 minutes. Splash in the Cognac and ignite, making sure you stand well back.
2  When the flames have died down, stir in the tarragon, salt, pepper and crème fraîche. Heat through gently until the crème fraîche has formed a sauce.
3  Divide among six small bowls and serve with crusty baguettes to mop up the juices, finger bowls and a pile of napkins.

• Per serving 146 kcalories, protein 15g, carbohydrate 2g, fat 8g, saturated fat 3g, fibre none, added sugar none, salt 1.53g

These fragrant and tasty peppers are great either on their own, or thrown into pasta or perched on top of pizza. They will keep in a sealed jar in the fridge for up to a week.

# Smoky Paprika Peppers

500ml mild olive oil
2 tsp sweet smoked paprika
(available in most supermarkets)
1 garlic clove, peeled and thinly sliced
1 tbsp black peppercorns
1 tbsp fennel seed
8 red peppers, halved
8 yellow peppers, halved
pinch of salt
300ml/½ pt white wine vinegar
small handful of fresh flatleaf parsley leaves, chopped (optional)

Takes 40 minutes • Makes enough to fill 3 x 500ml jars

1  Pour the oil into a pan. Add the paprika and garlic. Heat very gently for 5 minutes, cool and strain through a muslin-lined sieve. In another pan, dry fry the spices for 1 minute. Add to the paprika oil and set aside.

2  Heat the grill to high. Spread the peppers over 2 large baking sheets, skin-side up. Grill for about 15 minutes, or until the skins are blackened. Transfer to plastic food bags, seal and cool. When the peppers are cool enough to handle, discard the skins, stalks and seeds and tear the peppers into large pieces.

3  Tip the peppers, vinegar and a little salt into 300m/½ pint simmering water in a large pan. Return to a simmer for 3 minutes, drain well. Mix in the parsley (if using) and pack into jars. Gently reheat the spiced oil for a few minutes, pour over the peppers and seal.

• Undrained, per jar 1585 kcalories, protein 8.4g, carbohydrate 44.2g, fat 154g, saturated fat 21.3g, fibre 21.3g, sugar 41.8g, salt 1.08g

An excellent prepare-ahead party nibble; all the elements can be made in advance then put together half an hour before your guests arrive.

# Tomato and Feta Pesto Bites

½ x 350g pack puff pastry (the rest can be frozen to use another time)
25g/1oz Parmesan, finely grated
20g pack fresh flatleaf parsley
2 tbsp pine nuts
100g/4oz feta, crumbled
1 garlic clove, peeled and crushed
4 tbsp olive oil

TO SERVE
12 small cherry tomatoes, halved
black olives, pitted

Takes 40–45 minutes, plus 20 minutes chilling • Makes 12

1  Roll out the pastry on a surface lightly dusted with the Parmesan (to about the thickness of a 10-pence piece). Stamp out 12 rounds using a 6cm/2½in plain cutter and line a shallow, 12-hole bun tin. Chill for 20 minutes. Pre-heat the oven to 200°C/Gas 6/fan 180°C.
2  Prick each pastry base and bake for 15–20 minutes until golden. Remove from the tin and cool on a wire rack. Meanwhile, tear the leaves from the parsley stalks and put all but 12 of the small sprigs in a food processor with the pine nuts, then whiz until coarsely chopped. Add the feta, garlic and oil and whiz to a thick paste.
3  To serve, dollop a spoonful of the feta pesto on to the tarts and top each one with two cherry-tomato halves. Garnish with reserved parsley sprigs. Serve with olives.

• Per serving 271 kcalories, protein 7g, carbohydrate 11g, fat 22g, saturated fat 8g, fibre none, added sugar none, salt 0.96g

This simple, no-cook nibble looks impressive and is packed with Mediterranean textures and flavours.

# Summer Deli Platter

250g tub ricotta
handful of chives
4 sun-dried tomatoes, finely chopped
selection of vegetables from deli counter, such as roasted aubergines and peppers, artichoke hearts, olives and balsamic red onions
toasted pittas or breadsticks, to serve

Takes 10 minutes • Serves 4

1 Tip the ricotta into a bowl and stir to soften it. Snip in the chives.
2 Add the sundried tomatoes, season to taste, then stir well.
3 Put the deli veg on to a platter with the toasted pittas or breadsticks and serve with the dip.

• Per serving 351 kcalories, protein 9g, carbohydrate 17g, fat 28g, saturated fat 7g, fibre 6g, sugar 9g, salt 5.65g

The flavours work really well when served with triangles of toasted pitta bread, houmous and fresh mint. Will keep in the fridge for up to a week.

# Aubergines and Feta with Chilli

8 large aubergines
500g box sea salt flakes (you only need about ⅓ box)
200ml/7fl oz red wine vinegar
500ml bottle light olive oil
3 tsp dried oregano
1 tsp chilli flakes
2 tsp black peppercorns
200g pack feta, drained, cut into cubes

Takes 1 hour, plus overnight salting • Makes enough to fill 3 x 500ml jars

1 The night before, slice the aubergines lengthways (about depth of a £1 coin). Layer the slices in a colander, sprinkle with salt and cover with cling film. Sit the colander over a bowl and leave in the fridge overnight.
2 Discard the juice from the aubergines. Bring the vinegar to the boil with an equal quantity of cold water. Add the aubergines, return to the boil, then turn down and simmer for 3 minutes until tender. Drain and pat dry.
3 Heat a griddle pan. Brush the aubergine strips with a little oil on both sides, cook (in batches) for 2 minutes each side, until charred. Heat oil, oregano, chilli and peppercorns in a pan over a low heat until warm – not too hot. Pack the aubergines and cheese into jars, top up with the herby oil. Seal in jars, leave to cool.

• Undrained, per jar 1710 kcalories, protein 20.6g, carbohydrate 27.4g, fat 169.5g, saturated fat 29.7g, fibre 21.3g, sugar 22.7g, salt 57.76g

Try to get the small chorizo sausages from the deli counter to cut into chunky slices, or buy slicing chorizo that can be cut into cubes.

# Flamed Chorizo

**FOR THE PATATAS BRAVAS**
5 tbsp olive oil
1 small onion, peeled and chopped
2 garlic cloves, peeled and chopped
227g can chopped tomatoes
1 tbsp tomato purée
2 tsp sweet paprika (pimentón)
good pinch of chilli powder
900g/2lb potatoes, cut into small cubes
chopped fresh flatleaf parsley, to garnish

**FOR THE CHORIZO**
200–300g/8–10oz chunky chorizo, sliced or cubed
3 tbsp vodka

Takes about 1 hour 15 mins • Serves 10–12 as part of a tapas

1  Fry the onion in three tablespoons of oil in a pan for about 5 minutes or until softened. Add the garlic, tomatoes, tomato purée, paprika, chilli powder and a little sugar and salt to taste. Bring to boil, stirring. Simmer for 10 minutes until pulpy. Set aside.

2  Pre-heat the oven to 200°C /Gas 6/fan 180°C. Spread the potatoes in a roasting tin, toss in the remaining oil and season. Roast for 40–50 minutes until crisp and golden. Reheat the sauce, tip the potatoes into dishes and spoon over the sauce. Sprinkle with parsley.

3  Put the chorizo into a flameproof dish. Pour over the vodka and carefully ignite. When the flames have died down, serve with the patatas bravas and cocktail sticks for spearing.

• Per portion 197 kcalories, protein 6.2g, carbohydrate 18.1g, fat 10.5g, saturated fat 2.6g, fibre 1.6g, sugar 2.2g, salt 0.37g

These simple skewers are good roasted in the oven, but they are also brilliant grilled or barbecued.

# Steak and Prosciutto Skewers

3 lemons, each cut into 8 wedges
36 fresh bay leaves
12 slices prosciutto, halved crossways
6 thick slices coarse-textured bread, such as a country loaf, each cut into 4 rough chunks
4 thick fillet steaks, each cut into 6 big cubes
olive oil, for drizzling
handful of fresh sage and thyme, finely chopped (optional)

Takes 20–30 minutes • Serves 6

1  Pre-heat the oven to 220°C/Gas 7/fan 200°C. Thread the ingredients on to skewers; for the tastiest results, do it in the following order: lemon, bay leaf, prosciutto, bread, steak, lemon, bay leaf, prosciutto, bread, steak, bay leaf – you will have 12 skewers.
2  Put them on a baking sheet and drizzle with olive oil. (You can prepare them a day ahead and keep in the fridge, if you wish.)
3  Sprinkle with the sage and thyme and some seasoning if you want. Roast for 5 minutes then turn and cook a further 3 minutes or until the bread is crisp and the steak is cooked.

• Per serving 353 kcalories, protein 36g, carbohydrate 27g, fat 12g, saturated fat 4g, fibre 1g, added sugar none, salt 1.47g

A traditional Italian way to cook fish – perfect for alfresco entertaining.

# Baked Fish on Rosemary Potatoes

1 large fennel bulb, roughly chopped
6 medium-sized potatoes, peeled and sliced thinly
8 tbsp olive oil
8 garlic cloves
8 fresh rosemary sprigs
2–3 whole fish such as bream, bass, trout or grey mullet (about 1.5kg/3lb total weight), gutted and scaled
2 x 275g packets cherry tomatoes on the vine
green salad, to serve

Takes 1–1 hour 20 minutes • Serves 6

1 Blanch the fennel for 1 minute. Drain. Pre-heat the oven to 190°C/Gas 5/fan 170°C. Put the potato slices and fennel in a large roasting tin, pour three-quarters of the oil over. Bash four of garlic cloves, skins still on. Season the potatoes, add the garlic and four broken-up sprigs of rosemary. Gently toss all together to coat in olive oil. Arrange in a thin layer in the pan, bake for 15 minutes.
2 Peel, bash and slice remaining garlic. Make three slashes across each fish and insert the garlic slices. Season inside and out. Drizzle oil over the fish and rub it in. Remove the potatoes after 15 minutes and lay the fish on top with the sprigs of tomatoes.
3 Give a final drizzle of oil. Roast until the potatoes and the fish are cooked through, about 25–35 minutes. Serve with a salad.

• Per serving 495 kcalories, protein 48g, carbohydrate 26g, fat 23g, saturated fat 3g, fibre 4g, added sugar none, salt 0.77g

Celebrate the arrival of summer and light the barbecue for this zesty and aromatic pork dish.

# Barbecued Pork with Sage and Lemon

85g/3oz pack prosciutto
finely grated zest and juice
3 lemons
3 tbsp roughly chopped fresh sage
leaves
3 x 350–450g/12oz–1lb pork
tenderloins, trimmed of any fat
oil, for brushing
50g/2oz butter, chilled and cut into
thin slices
fresh sage sprigs, to garnish

Takes 40–50 minutes • Serves 8

1  Whiz together the prosciutto, the zest of three and juice from 1½ lemons, chopped sage and seasoning to make a thick paste. Put aside and reserve the remaining lemons.
2  Make a deep cut lengthways through the centre of each tenderloin. Open out the meat, butterfly style, and flatten slightly. Make 10 deep slashes in each tenderloin. Rub paste over the meat, working it into the slashes.
3  Brush the tenderloins with oil. Barbecue the meat, paste-side down, for 6–8 minutes. Turn over, cook a further 6–8 minutes until cooked through. Transfer the pork to a platter. While hot, top with the slices of butter. Leave for a minute to melt. Squeeze the reserved lemon over the pork. Scatter with sage and serve cut into thick slices.

• Per serving 255 kcalories, protein 32g, carbohydrate 1g, fat 13.6g, saturated fat 6g, fibre none, added sugar none, salt 0.62g

This is just one of numerous variations of this Sicilian potato cake – torta di patate – a staple in many a trattoria. It's delicious eaten warm.

# Sicilian Potato Cake

1.3kg/3lb floury potatoes, such as King Edward or Maris Piper, left whole, skins on
175g/6oz pancetta, diced
250ml/9fl oz milk
100g/4oz unsalted butter
4 eggs, beaten
2 garlic cloves, peeled and crushed
200g/8oz Parmesan, freshly grated
6 slices Italian salami, chopped
85g/3oz provolone or caciocavallo cheese, diced
140g/5oz mozzarella, diced
handful of flatleaf parsley, chopped
50g/2oz fresh white breadcrumbs
handful of fresh thyme leaves

Takes about 2 hours • Cuts into 12 slices

1 Pre-heat the oven to 190°C/Gas 5/fan 170°C. Simmer the potatoes until tender – about 30–40 minutes. Fry the pancetta until golden. Drain, peel and cut the potatoes into chunks. Tip back into the pan with the milk and most of the butter. Mash well. Mix in the pancetta and all ingredients except the breadcrumbs and thyme.

2 Butter a 23cm/9in springform tin. Coat the inside with about three-quarters of the breadcrumbs and fill with the potato mixture. Smooth the surface and press the remaining breadcrumbs gently into the potato.

3 Bake for 1 hour 10 minutes until the potato cake is set, with a slight wobble in the middle. Let it rest for 5 minutes then loosen from the sides before releasing. Slide on to a plate and sprinkle with thyme leaves.

• Per serving 381 kcalories, protein 20g, carbohydrate 22g, fat 24g, saturated fat 13g, fibre 1g, added sugar none, salt 1.86g

Using a barbecue is a wonderful way of cooking paella. You need a large paella pan for this (about 40cm/16in across) or a large, wide frying pan with fairly deep sides.

# Paella on the Barbecue

2 litres/3½ pints vegetable or chicken stock
good pinch of saffron strands
4 tbsp olive oil
100g/4oz chorizo sausage, thinly sliced
450g/1lb boneless skinless chicken breasts or thighs, cut into cubes
1 onion, peeled and chopped into small dice
3 garlic cloves, peeled and finely chopped
450g/1lb ripe tomatoes, chopped
1 red pepper, seeded and chopped
200g/8oz green beans, trimmed and halved
2 tsp paprika
450g/1lb short grain rice, such as calasparra or arborio
300g/12oz large raw prawns in shells
large handful of flatleaf parsley, roughly chopped
lemon wedges, to serve

Takes 50 minutes–1 hour 5 minutes
Serve 6

1 Prepare the barbecue. Bring the stock and saffron to a simmer in a pan. Set a paella or large frying pan on the barbecue and heat half the oil in it. Add the chorizo and fry until crisp, then transfer to a plate.

2 Add the remaining oil to the pan. Fry the chicken, stirring, until lightly coloured. Add the onion and garlic and stir fry for 3–4 minutes. Stir in the tomatoes and pepper. Season, stir in the beans and paprika. Stir in the rice until the grains begin to soak up the oil. Add two ladlefuls of hot stock. When it bubbles, stir in more. Continue adding stock and stirring for 15 minutes, or until the rice is just tender.

3 Return the chorizo to the pan. Add the prawns and until they turn pink (2-3mins). Season. Remove from the heat, cover with foil. Let it cool for 5 minutes, stir in the parsley.

• Per portion 525 kcalories, protein 34.5g, carbohydrate 69.7g, fat 13.9g, saturated fat 3.0g, fibre 5.3g, sugar 8.7g, salt 0.94g

The name pissaladière comes from *pissalat*, the Provençal word for a purée of anchovies. For an authentic touch, drizzle the pissaladière with extra olive oil straight after baking.

# Pissaladière

### FOR THE DOUGH

200g/8oz strong white bread flour
1 tsp salt
2 tsp easy-blend dried yeast
150ml/¼ pint warm water
1 tbsp olive oil

### FOR THE TOPPING

4 tbsp olive oil, plus extra
for drizzling
1kg/2lb 4oz onions, peeled and
thinly sliced
few fresh thyme sprigs
2 tomatoes, skinned and chopped
2 x 80g cans anchovy fillets, drained,
any fat ones halved lengthways
handful of black olives, pitted

Takes 2–2¼ hours • Serves 6–8

1  Tip the flour, salt and yeast into a bowl. Add the water and oil. Mix to a soft dough. Knead on a lightly floured surface for 5 minutes. Return the dough to the bowl, cover, and let rise for 45 minutes to 1¼ hours.
2  Heat the oil in a pan, fry the onions gently, for about 10 minutes until softened, not browned. Stir in the thyme and tomatoes and season. Cover and cook gently for 45 minutes until the onions are meltingly soft, stirring occasionally and removing the lid for the last 10 minutes. Remove, let cool slightly.
3  Pre-heat the oven to 220°C/Gas 7/fan 200°C. Lightly oil a shallow 23x33cm/9x13in baking sheet. Knead the dough briefly, roll it out, press into the tin. Spread the onion mixture over, arrange the anchovies on top in a criss-cross pattern. Add olives and bake for 25–30 minutes until golden.

• Per serving for six 400 kcals, protein 13g, fat 15g, saturated fat 1.4g, carbohydrate 30g, added sugar none, fibre 4g ,salt 3.4g

These succulent chicken parcels are just the thing for eating outside on a summer's day. Serve with a simple salad.

# Tarragon and Almond Chicken

4 boneless skinless chicken breasts
50g/2oz slightly salted butter, softened
1 tsp finely chopped fresh tarragon, plus extra for garnishing
1 tsp finely chopped fresh parsley
½ tsp finely snipped fresh chives
25g/1oz ground almonds
4 large thin slices prosciutto

Takes 40–50 minutes • Serves 4

1  Pre-heat the oven to 200°C/Gas 6/fan 180°C. Pat each chicken breast dry with kitchen paper. Make three lengthways slits in the top of each breast, cutting halfway through the meat. Cream the butter and herbs until smooth, blend in the almonds and a pinch of salt. Divide into four and spread in to the slits in each breast.

2  Wrap the prosciutto around each breast, overlapping the ends. Lay the parcels in an oiled ovenproof dish, cover loosely with buttered greaseproof paper or foil.

3  Bake the chicken for 20 minutes. Remove the butter paper or foil for the last 5 minutes. Allow the chicken to cool for 5 minutes, then transfer to plates and spoon over the melted butter that has collected in the bottom of the dish. Garnish with extra tarragon.

• Per serving 311 kcalories, protein 39g, carbohydrate 1g, fat 17g, saturated fat 8g, fibre 1g, added sugar none, salt 1.05g

Perk up your pasta and taste the sunshine flavours in this Spanish-style tagliatelle.

# Seafood Tagliatelle Spanish-style

large pinch of saffron strands
3 tbsp olive oil
3 boneless skinless chicken breasts, cut into small chunks
1 medium onion, peeled and finely chopped
2 garlic cloves, peeled and crushed
2 bay leaves
2 red peppers, seeded and sliced
175g/6oz fresh or frozen peas
175g/6oz fresh or frozen broad beans
150ml/¼ pint white wine
650g/1lb 7oz fresh mussels
425ml/¾ pint chicken stock
400g/14oz tagliatelle
450g/1lb large raw peeled prawns
284ml carton double cream
large handful of chopped fresh parsley
lemon wedges and bread, to serve

Takes 50–60 minutes • Serves 6

1  Put the saffron and two tablespoons of boiling water in a bowl. Set aside. Heat oil in a pan, add the chicken and cook for 4–5 minutes. Tip in the onion and garlic, cook for 3–4 minutes. Add bay leaves and peppers, cook for 4–5 minutes. Add peas and broad beans, and cook for 2–3 minutes. Set aside.
2  Pour the wine into a large pan, bring to a simmer. Tip in the mussels, cover and cook for 3–5 minutes. Discard any that don't open. Drain and reserve the liquid. Pour the liquid into the pan with the chicken and veg. Add saffron and chicken stock.
3  Cook the tagliatelle according to the packet instructions. Simmer the chicken for 2 minutes. Add the prawns, cook for 1 minute; add the cream, cook for 2–3 minutes. Add the mussels, parsley and season. When hot, drain the tagliatelle and tip into the sauce.

• Per serving 724 kcalories, protein 49g, carbohydrate 57g, fat 33g, saturated fat 16g, fibre 6g, added sugar none, salt 3.54g

This tart uses the light Mediterranean flavours of peppers, olives and tomatoes that work so well with goats' cheese. A great dish to share with family or friends.

# Goats' Cheese and Red Pepper Tart

2 large red onions, peeled and thinly sliced
2 tbsp olive oil
1 tbsp balsamic vinegar
12 black olives, pitted and roughly chopped
2 red peppers (choose tapered, heart-shaped ones if possible), halved, seeded and cored
200g/8oz ready-made shortcrust pastry
150–200g log firm goats' cheese, such as Sainte-Maure de Touraine or 150–200g drum of Capricorn, sliced
250g/9oz cherry tomatoes
few fresh oregano or basil leaves

Takes about 1 hour • Serves 4–6

1  Cook the onions in oil for 6–7 minutes, until golden. Add the vinegar and one tablespoon of water. Cook for 2–3 minutes. Stir in the olives, cool. Grill peppers until skins are charred. Put into a plastic food bag until cool enough to handle. Remove skins.
2  Pre-heat the oven to 200°C/Gas 6/fan 180°C. Roll out the pastry and line a 23–24cm/9–9½in flan tin. Line with baking paper and beans; bake for 10 minutes. Remove paper and beans; bake for 5 minutes more.
3  Spread the onion mix over the pastry base. Lay the peppers on top, cut-side up, with tapered ends towards the centre. Put a few slices of goats' cheese in each pepper half. Tuck the tomatoes among the peppers. Bake for 20–25 minutes until the cheese is lightly browned and the tomatoes have burst. Scatter over the herb leaves.

• Per serving for four 471 kcalories, protein 13g, carbohydrate 37g, fat 31g, saturated fat 13g, fibre 4g, sugar 12g, salt 1.35g

A new and very tasty take on barbecuing.

# Pan-roasted Chicken with Crisp Prosciutto

100g/4oz soft butter
4 garlic cloves, peeled and chopped
2 tbsp olive oil
6 slices prosciutto (85g pack)
6 x 175g/6oz boneless skinless
chicken breasts
2 x 400g cans chopped tomatoes
150ml/¼ pint chicken or vegetable
stock
4 fresh oregano sprigs, leaves
removed and chopped
400g can cannellini beans, drained
and rinsed
1 ciabatta loaf, cut into 12 slices
250g punnet cherry tomatoes, halved
18 fresh basil leaves, half chopped,
half left whole
mixed salad leaves tossed in your
favourite dressing, to serve

Takes 50 minutes–1 hour • Serves 6

1  Prepare the barbecue. Mix the butter with half the garlic. Heat a sturdy roasting tin on the barbecue, drizzle in the oil. Lay in the prosciutto and crisp it on both sides. Set aside. Season the chicken, brown on both sides in the tin. Stir in the remaining chopped garlic, chopped tomatoes, stock and oregano. Simmer for 3 minutes, turn the breasts over, simmer for another 3 minutes.
2  Tip in the beans, turn the chicken over and simmer for 3 minutes, turn again and simmer for 3 minutes more. Season. When the chicken is nearly done, toast the ciabatta.
3  Toss tomatoes and chopped basil into the chicken mix. Let the tomatoes soften, then top with crisp prosciutto and basil leaves. Spread the garlic butter on the ciabatta and arrange, butter-side up, around the edge of the chicken. Serve with a mixed leaf salad.

• Per serving 550 kcalories, protein 54.5g, carbohydrate 32g, fat 23g, saturated fat 11g, fibre 5g, added sugar none, salt 2.59g

A hearty, fragrantly spiced Mediterranean sandwich. The lamb steaks can also be cooked on the barbecue for a really rustic flavour.

# Turkish-style Lamb

4 lamb leg steaks
1 tsp each ground cumin and coriander
1 garlic clove, peeled and crushed
1 tsp dried oregano or mixed herbs
small bunch fresh mint, leaves only, chopped
2 x 150g cartons low-fat, natural yoghurt
4 pitta breads, white or wholemeal
½ iceberg lettuce
1 red onion
1 lemon, cut into wedges, for squeezing (optional)

Takes 20 minutes • Serves 4

1 Heat the grill to high. Season the lamb with salt and pepper and grill for 2 minutes on each side until browned, but still very rare. Meanwhile, mix the cumin, coriander, garlic, oregano and half of the mint into one of the cartons of yoghurt. Smother this over the lamb, then return to the grill for another 2–3 minutes or until the yoghurt is blistered and the meat is cooked to your liking.

2 Leave the meat to rest on a board for a few minutes while you toast the pittas, shred the lettuce and peel and thinly slice the red onion. Stir the rest of the mint into the second carton of yoghurt.

3 Thickly slice the meat and stuff into the pitta bread with the salad and minted yoghurt. Squeeze over lemon juice before tucking in, if you like.

• Per serving 502 kcalories, protein 48g, carbohydrate 51g, fat 13g, saturated fat 6g, fibre 3g, sugar 9g, salt 1.53g

*Succulent skewers bursting with the flavours of Provence.*
*Let the weather decide whether you grill, griddle or barbecue.*

# Provençal Pork Skewers

600g/1lb 5oz pork fillet
1 bunch spring onions
2 tsp dried herbes de Provence
finely grated zest and juice 1 lemon
1 tbsp clear honey
1 tbsp olive oil

Takes about 16–20 minutes • Serves 4

1  Cut the pork into bite-sized chunks and cut the spring onions into 3cm/1¼in lengths.
2  In a bowl, mix together the herbs, lemon zest and juice, honey, oil and a little seasoning. Add the pork and onions and stir well to coat all the pieces of meat evenly.
3  Thread the meat and onion alternately on to four or eight skewers. Heat a griddle pan or grill until hot. Cook the skewers for 6–8 minutes, turning occasionally, until browned.

• Per serving 220 kcalories, protein 38g, carbohydrate 3g, fat 6g, saturated fat 2g, fibre none, sugar 2g, salt 0.2g

Serve this quick, one-pan dish with rice or for a speedier supper, with couscous or lightly toasted pitta bread.

# Moroccan Lamb Pan-fry

1 bunch chard
1 tbsp olive oil
600g/1lb 5oz diced shoulder of lamb
1 onion, peeled and sliced
2 garlic cloves, peeled and sliced
1 tsp each ground turmeric, cumin and coriander seeds
pinch of chilli flakes
400ml/14fl oz lamb or chicken stock
handful of raisins
handful of toasted pine nuts, to serve

Takes 30 minutes • Serves 4

1 Strip the chard leaves from the stalks. Cut the stalks into batons and roughly shred the leaves. Set aside separately.
2 Heat the oil in a frying pan and fry the lamb for 5–6 minutes over a high heat until browned. Add the onion, garlic, chard stalks and spices and continue to cook for 3–4 minutes until softened. Pour over the stock and scatter in the raisins, then simmer for 4–5 minutes to make a sauce.
3 Stir the chard leaves through the stock to wilt, season and serve garnished with the pine nuts.

• Per serving 438 kcalories, protein 38g, carbohydrate 12g, fat 27g, saturated fat 10.04g, fibre 0.8g, sugar 7.7g, salt 1g

Ready in minutes, this meal is the perfect way to end
a busy day.

# Balsamic Pork with Olives

3 tbsp olive oil
3 tbsp balsamic vinegar
1 tsp Dijon mustard
2 garlic cloves, peeled and crushed
4 boneless pork loin chops
2 handfuls of green olives, pitted and halved
large handful of fresh basil, chopped
cooked pasta, to serve

Takes 20 minutes • Serves 4

1  Mix the oil with vinegar, mustard and garlic. Score the meat on both sides, season, then put into a dish. Pour over the balsamic mixture and leave to marinate for 5 minutes.
2  Heat a griddle pan until very hot. Lift the pork from the marinade, scraping off any garlic, then reserve the marinade. Cook the pork for 4 minutes on each side. Remove the meat and keep warm.
3  Pour the marinade into the pan with the olives, cook for 2 minutes, then stir in the basil. Pour any juices from the pork into the pan, drizzle the sauce over the pork and serve with pasta.

• Per serving 487 kcalories, protein 27g, carbohydrate 2g, fat 41g, saturated fat 13g, fibre 1g, sugar 2g, salt 0.51g

A luxurious combination of chicken, prosciutto and creamy sauce makes this an easy yet impressive dish for midweek entertaining. Serve with a little fresh pasta.

# Chicken with Prosciutto and Fried Sage

2 boneless skinless chicken breasts
4 slices prosciutto
1 tbsp plain flour
1 tbsp olive oil
handful of fresh sage leaves
25g/1oz butter
150ml/¼ pint dry white wine
4 tbsp double cream or crème fraîche

Takes 20 minutes • Serves 2

1  Beat the chicken breasts between two sheets of greaseproof paper with a rolling pin until about twice the original size. Lay two rippled slices of prosciutto on top of each breast and secure with a cocktail stick. Dust each breast lightly with flour, season and set aside.

2  Heat the oil in a frying pan and fry the sage leaves for about 30 seconds until just crisp. Remove and drain on kitchen paper. Add the butter to the pan and fry the chicken for 3–4 minutes on each side until browned.

3  Remove the chicken and set aside. Stir in the wine, scraping all the bits from the base of the pan. Reduce by about half. Stir in the cream or crème fraîche, return the chicken to the pan and heat through. Scatter in the fried sage leaves and serve.

• Per serving 667 kcalories, protein 34g, carbohydrate 14g, fat 48g, saturated fat 20g, fibre trace, added sugar none, salt 1.96g

A delicious and comforting dish that takes only minutes
to prepare.

# Pork with Crème Fraîche and Prunes

2 pork fillets (about 500g/1lb 2oz total weight), thickly sliced into medallions
2 tbsp plain flour, seasoned
25g/1oz butter
20 ready-to-eat pitted prunes
2 tbsp brandy
300ml/½ pint white wine
1 tbsp Dijon mustard
1 tbsp redcurrant jelly
200ml carton crème fraîche
tagliatelle and broccoli or green salad, to serve

Takes 25 minutes • Serves 4

1  Dust the pork with a little of the seasoned flour. Heat the butter in a large non-stick frying pan, then cook the pork in batches for about 3 minutes on each side.
2  Remove from the pan then add the prunes, brandy, wine, mustard and redcurrant jelly and simmer to reduce the mixture by half.
3  Stir in the crème fraîche to make a creamy sauce, season well, then return the pork to the pan to heat through. Serve with tagliatelle and broccoli or a green salad.

• Per serving 600 kcalories, protein 31g, carbohydrate 35g, fat 34g, saturated fat 19g, fibre 4g, sugar 28g, salt 0.85g

Whenever you buy fish, try to get sustainably caught. This dish goes well with wilted spinach and potatoes.

# Lemon Sole Baked with Grapes

50g/1oz butter
2 whole lemon soles, skin removed
2 handfuls of white seedless grapes
1 glass white wine

Takes 30 minutes • Serves 2

1 Pre-heat the oven to 210°C/Gas 7/fan 190°C. Use half the butter to grease a large ovenproof dish, then slip in the soles, scatter over the grapes and pour over a drizzle of wine.
2 Bake the fish for 15–20 minutes until cooked and the flesh is coming away from the bone.
3 Using a fish slice, carefully lift the fish on to plates and place the ovenproof dish on the heat. Pour over the remaining wine and bubble everything together for 4–5 minutes until reduced and sticky. Swirl in the remaining butter, check the seasoning, then pour over the fish.

• Per serving 401 kcalories, protein 33g, carbohydrate 4g, fat 24g, saturated fat 14g, fibre none, sugar 4g, salt 0.85g

If you haven't got any grappa you can use white wine instead.

# Roast Chicken with Grappa

100g/4oz plain flour
2 good pinches of saffron strands,
crushed in a pestle and mortar
6 chicken breasts, bone in and
skin on
6 tbsp extra virgin olive oil
4 large sweet potatoes, about
1.5 kg/3lb 5oz, peeled and cut
into large chunks
150ml/¼ pint full-fat milk
140g/5oz Taleggio cheese, broken
into chunks
8 tbsp grappa (Italian brandy)
4 handfuls of seedless red grapes

Takes 40–45 minutes • Serves 6

1  Pre-heat the oven to 200°C/Gas 6/fan 180°C. Mix together the flour and saffron. Coat the chicken, shaking off any excess. Heat oil in a roasting tin and brown the chicken all over. Cover with foil and roast for 20 minutes until the chicken is crisp. Remove the foil for the final 5 minutes of cooking.
2  Boil the potatoes until tender, about 15 minutes, drain and mash. Return the pan to a low heat, season, then stir in the milk and Taleggio until smooth and creamy.
3  When the chicken is cooked, put the tin on the hob and add the grappa and grapes. Warm through, remove from the heat and flambé. When the flames die down, simmer for 30 seconds. Serve the chicken on top of the mash with grapes sauce spooned over.

• Per serving 689 kcalories, protein 43g, carbohydrate 71g, fat 23g, saturated fat 8g, fibre 7g, added sugar none, salt 1.44g

A mouth-watering fish Mediterranean dish. Serve with wedges of garlicky roast potatoes.

# Italian Fish and Garlic Tomatoes

2 unpeeled garlic cloves
3 tbsp olive oil
100g/4oz black unpitted olives
900g/2lb tomatoes, preferably on the vine
2 medium red chillies, seeded and roughly chopped
3 tbsp fresh pesto sauce
2 boneless skinless cod fillets (about 450g/1lb each), from a sustainable source
finely grated zest 1 small lemon
12 slices prosciutto

Takes about 1 hour 5 minutes
Serves 6

1 Pre-heat the oven to 200°C/Gas 6/fan 180°C. Put the garlic in a roasting tin with two tablespoons of oil. Roast for 15 minutes, then remove from the oven and set aside. Add the olives, tomatoes and chillies to the tin and stir.

2 Spread the pesto over one side of a cod fillet, sprinkle over lemon zest, season. Lay the other cod fillet on top, then loosely wrap the prosciutto around the fish, tucking in the edges. Season with salt and drizzle over remaining oil. Put the cod on a rack over the roasting tin and roast for 20 minutes or until fish is cooked and the tomatoes are starting to break up.

3 Transfer the cod to a plate. Mash the garlic into the pan juices and discard the skins. Slice the cod and serve with the olives, tomatoes, chillies and pan juices.

• Per serving 326 kcalories, protein 40g, carbohydrate 5g, fat 16g, saturated fat 3g, fibre 2g, added sugar none, salt 3.12g

Try to pick smallish poussins for this. The orange and sherry make terrific pan juices to drizzle over the birds for serving.

# Roasted Poussin with Oregano, Orange and Sherry

4 poussins
2 tbsp olive oil
2 tsp dried oregano
2 oranges
4 tbsp medium or dry sherry

Takes 45–50 minutes • Serves 4

1 Pre-heat the oven to 190°C/Gas 5/fan 170°C. Put the poussin in a roasting tin, drizzle with the oil, sprinkle over the oregano and season with some salt and pepper.
2 Roast for 15 minutes, then add the finely grated zest from one of the oranges and squeeze the juice from both. Pour over the birds with the sherry.
3 Return to the oven and roast for a further 20–25 minutes or until cooked.

• Per serving 549 kcalories, protein 45g, carbohydrate 4g, fat 38g, saturated fat 10g, fibre none, added sugar none, salt 0.67g

The preparation of this dish for one is simple and while the lamb simmers away in the oven, you can sit back, relax, pour yourself a glass of wine and think of sunny Greece.

# Slow Roasted Greek-style Lamb

2 tbsp olive oil
1 lamb shank (about 400g/14oz)
1 small red onion, peeled, halved and thickly sliced
1 medium potato, peeled and quartered
4 garlic cloves, peeled and left whole
4 fresh rosemary sprigs
1 tbsp tomato purée
230g can chopped tomatoes
125ml/4fl oz white wine
crusty bread, to serve

Takes about 2 hours • Serves 1

1  Heat the oil in a small casserole dish or ovenproof pan with a lid. Season the lamb shank with salt and pepper and fry in the hot oil for 10 minutes, turning often to brown it all over. Remove from the dish and set aside.
2  Pre-heat the oven to 180°C/Gas 4/fan 160°C. Fry the onion slices in the same oil as the lamb for about 8 minutes until they start to colour, then stir in the potato, garlic and rosemary and continue to cook for another 2 minutes so that everything is coated in the oil.
3  Stir in the tomato purée, tomatoes and white wine, season and bring to a simmer. Nestle the lamb shank in the mixture, cover and place in the oven. Cook for 1½ hours or until the lamb is very tender, turning once halfway through cooking. Serve with crusty bread.

• Per serving 538 kcalories, protein 34g, carbohydrate 19g, fat 34g, saturated fat 12g, fibre 3g, added sugar none, salt 0.52g

The quality of the wine makes all the difference in this recipe, so only use one that you'd be happy to drink.

# Italian Chicken with Basil and Beans

8 skinless chicken thighs, bone in
large bunch fresh basil
8 slices prosciutto or other dry-cured ham
2 tbsp olive oil
800g/1lb 12oz tomatoes (a mix of smaller yellow and red tomatoes looks good), halved or quartered, depending on size
2 whole heads garlic, halved around the middle
175ml/6oz dry white wine, preferably Italian
400g can cannellini or other white beans, drained and rinsed

Takes 1 hour 25 minutes • Serves 4 generously

1  Season the chicken. Lay a basil sprig on each chicken thigh amd wrap in a piece of ham, tucking the ends underneath. Pre-heat the oven to 160°C/Gas 3/fan 140°C. Heat oil in a large roasting tin on the hob. Add the chicken and fry for 4 minutes or until the ham is crisp and the chicken is lightly golden.
2  Pick the leaves from the basil. Once the chicken has browned, add the tomatoes, garlic, wine and half the basil. Cover with foil and cook in the oven for 40 minutes.
3  Remove from oven and raise heat to 220°C/Gas 7/fan 200°C. Remove the foil and stir in the beans. Return to the oven, uncovered, for 30 minutes until the chicken is very tender. Just before serving, tear the remaining basil roughly and stir through.

• Per serving 455 kcalories, protein 55g, carbohydrate 22g, fat 16g, saturated fat 4g, fibre 6g, sugar 10g, salt 1.79g

A fascinating meat dish from Spain that combines the richness of dried fruit and nuts with other traditional Mediterranean ingredients.

# Braised Beef with Almonds, Prunes and Apricots

2 garlic cloves, peeled
3 tbsp fresh flatleaf parsley, chopped
1.3kg/3lb piece beef topside
2 tbsp plain flour, for coating
3 tbsp olive oil
1 medium onion, peeled and chopped
3 fresh thyme sprigs
200ml/7fl oz dry white wine
1 large tomato, chopped
85g/3oz whole blanched toasted almonds, coarsely ground
10 ready-to-eat dried prunes
10 ready-to-eat dried apricots
mashed potato and green salad, to serve

Takes about 2 hours • Serves 6

1  Pound the garlic and parsley in a pestle and mortar, then press all over the meat. Season with salt and lightly pat the flour on top to coat evenly.
2  Heat the olive oil in a large casserole dish and brown the meat. Stir in the onion, thyme and wine and cook over a medium heat for 10 minutes, stirring often. Stir in the tomato and ground almonds. Cover and cook over a low to medium heat for 1 hour 30 minutes.
3  Stir in the prunes and apricots and cook for a further 15 minutes, covered, until the meat is very tender and the sauce is thickened. (If the sauce is too thin, remove the beef and reduce the sauce a little over a medium heat.) Put the beef on a warm serving plate and spoon the sauce around. Serve with mashed potato and a green salad.

• Per portion 665 kcalories, protein 49.5g, carbohydrate 21.1g, fat 41.9g, saturated fat 13.8g, fibre 4.0g, sugar 16.1g, salt 0.40g

Printanière means spring-like, and this is a delightful dish to make when beans and peas are in season.

# Lamb Printanière

1 kg/2lb 4oz boned shoulder of lamb
4 shallots, peeled and quartered
butter and olive oil, for frying
1 bouquet garni
600ml/1pint stock
300ml/½ pint white wine
4 carrots, cut into sticks
500g/1lb 2oz tiny new potatoes
500g/1lb 2oz broad beans, podded
500g/1lb 2oz fresh peas, podded
3–4 tbsp crème fraîche
fresh chervil or parsley sprigs, to garnish

Takes about 3¼ hours • Serves 4–6

1 Cut the lamb into large chunks. Fry the shallots gently in the butter and olive oil until softened, but not browned. Remove with a slotted spoon. Fry the lamb until browned (you may need to do this in batches).
2 Add the bouquet garni, stock and wine and season with salt and pepper. Bring to the boil, then reduce to a gentle simmer, cover tightly and cook for 1½ hours. Add the carrots and potatoes and cook for a further 30 minutes. (This can be cooked a day ahead and kept in the fridge.)
3 Fish out the bouquet garni then add the broad beans and peas. Cook for 10 minutes, then season well and stir in the crème fraîche. Ladle into soup bowls and scatter over some chervil or parsley.

• Per serving 1005 kcalories, protein 64g, carbohydrate 55g, fat 58g, saturated fat 28g, fibre 17g, sugar 17g, salt 1.28g

This Spanish dish is best cooked in a heavy-based frying pan, to allow the sauce to combine and reduce as it should.

# Chicken in Garlic, Herb and Olive Sauce

225ml/8fl oz olive oil
2 small chickens, about 1.3kg/3lb each, cut into 8 pieces (skin on)
6 garlic cloves, peeled
1 tbsp fresh thyme leaves
3 bay leaves
300ml/½ pint dry white wine
12 Manzanilla green olives
mashed potato and frisée salad, to serve

Takes about 40 minutes • Serves 6

1  Heat the oil in a large, deep frying pan, then fry the chicken over a high heat for about 5 minutes on each side until browned.
2  Add the garlic, thyme and bay leaves, then pour in the wine – take care as it will splutter, so put the lid on quickly. Reduce the heat and simmer, covered, for 15–20 minutes until the chicken is tender. (Adding wine to hot oil produces an emulsion – lift the lid off carefully after 10 minutes, not before, to see if it is creamy. If it isn't, remove from the heat, add a little hot water and return to the heat to finish simmering.)
3  Season with salt. Stir in the olives and serve with mash and salad.

• Per portion 908 kcalories, protein 56.9g, carbohydrate 3.1g, fat 72.5g, saturated fat 16g, fibre 0.4g, sugar 2.3g, salt 0.87g

Slow-cooked lamb is tender and flavoursome, and it is delicious in this rich, slightly sweet sauce.

# Greek Lamb Stew with Feta

3 tbsp olive oil
700g/1½lb boned shoulder of lamb, cubed
1 large onion, peeled and sliced
1 garlic bulb, broken into cloves and peeled
1 tbsp dried oregano
1 aubergine, cubed
1 bay leaf
300ml/½ pint lamb or vegetable stock
2 x 400g cans chopped tomatoes
400g can chickpeas, drained
50g/2oz sultanas

FOR THE COUSCOUS
700ml/1¼ pints hot vegetable stock
450g/1lb couscous

FOR THE TOPPING
200g/8oz feta, crumbled
2–3 tbsp chopped fresh mint

Takes about 2 hours • Serves 8

1 Pre-heat the oven to 190°C/Gas 5/fan 170°C. Heat the oil in a large casserole dish and brown the lamb in batches until golden. Remove with a slotted spoon and set aside. Add the onion to the casserole and cook for 2–3 minutes until softened. Stir in the garlic cloves, oregano and aubergine. Cook for 3–4 minutes until golden.

2 Return the lamb and juices to the pan. Add the bay leaf, stock, tomatoes, chickpeas and sultanas and season. Cover and bake for about 1½ hours or until the lamb is tender. Just before serving, pour hot stock over the couscous. Cover and let stand for 5 minutes, then fluff up with a fork. Season.

3 Mix the feta and mint and put it in a bowl. Serve the lamb with the couscous and the feta, with some of the feta sprinkled on top.

• Per serving 533 kcalories, protein 28g, carbohydrate 45g, fat 28g, saturated fat 12g, fibre 4g, added sugar none, salt 1.96g

The dimpled apricots look charming left whole, but they can also be halved and stoned before poaching.

# Summery Provençal Apricots

1 x 75cl bottle dry, fruity rosé wine
175g/6oz golden caster sugar
1 vanilla pod, split open lengthways
with a sharp knife, then cut in 4
(keep the seeds inside)
700g/1lb 9oz ripe fresh apricots,
whole or halved and stoned
vanilla ice cream, to serve

Takes 35–45 minutes • Serves 4

1 Pour the wine into a pan, tip in the sugar then add the pieces of vanilla pod. Stir over a low heat until the sugar has dissolved. Add the apricots.

2 Cover and gently poach the apricots until just softened – about 15–20 minutes for whole fruit and 10–15 minutes for halves.

3 Lift the apricots out and put them in a bowl. Boil the liquid hard for 8–10 minutes to make a thin syrup. Pour over the apricots and leave to cool. Serve warm or cold, with a good vanilla ice cream and a piece of vanilla pod to decorate.

• Per serving 356 kcalories, protein 2g, carbohydrate 62g, fat none, saturated fat 3g, fibre 3g, added sugar 46g, salt 0.03g

Beautifully scented and cooling, granitas are halfway between a drink and a sorbet. If you don't have rosewater, use elderflower cordial instead.

# Fruity Granitas

**MELON AND ROSE GRANITA**
1 ripe melon, such as Ogen, halved and seeded
140g/5oz golden caster sugar
few drops of rosewater (elderflower cordial can be used instead)
fresh rose petals, to decorate (optional)

**LEMONADE GRANITA**
3 unwaxed lemons
140g/5oz golden caster sugar
lemon zest strips, to decorate

Takes 20 minutes plus freezing
Serves 4

1  For the melon and rose granita, purée the melon flesh, sugar and rosewater in a food processor. Add 600ml/1 pint water and blend until smooth. Rub the mixture through a sieve into a plastic container. Freeze for 3 hours, until partially frozen. Beat with a fork, then freeze again. Beat occasionally until icy and slushy. Alternatively, use an ice-cream machine. Serve decorated with rose petals.
2  For the lemonade granita, blend the lemons, sugar and 600ml/1 pint water in a food processor. Sieve into a bowl, pressing out the juice. Freeze in a shallow container. When frozen, break into chunks and blend until smooth. Freeze for 2 hours until icy. Decorate with lemon zest to serve.

• Melon and Rose per portion 170 kcalories, protein 1.1g, carbohydrates 43.6g, fat 0.3g, saturated fat 0g, fibre 1.7g, sugar 43.6g, salt 0.04g • Lemonade per portion 151 kcalories, protein 0.7g, carbohydrate 38.9g, fat 0.2g, saturated fat 0g, fibre 0g, added sugar 38.9g, salt 0.01g

This dish is prepared by open-freezing, which means it is frozen just until it is firm, without being wrapped. Then, when you do wrap it, it won't get squashed.

# Limoncello and Raspberry Semifreddo

### FOR THE SEMIFREDDO
100g/4oz fresh or frozen (thawed) raspberries
85g/3oz golden caster sugar
284ml carton double cream
4 tbsp limoncello
2 x 200ml cartons crème fraîche
extra raspberries, to decorate

### FOR THE COULIS
225g/8oz fresh or frozen (thawed) raspberries
2 tbsp golden caster sugar
2 tbsp limoncello

Takes 20–25 minutes, plus thawing and freezing • Serves 8

1 Line the base of a 1kg/2lb 4oz loaf tin with baking parchment. For the semifreddo, mash the raspberries and half the sugar in a bowl. In a separate bowl, softly whisk the cream, the rest of the sugar and the limoncello. Beat the crème fraîche briefly and fold into the mixture. Swirl in the mashed raspberries. Pour into the tin and smooth the top. For the coulis, mash the raspberries, sugar and limoncello and push through a sieve.
2 Open-freeze the semifreddo then cover with cling film and foil and freeze overnight until firm. (Can be frozen for up to 1 month.)
3 To serve, thaw the semifreddo in the fridge for 1 hour. Remove it from the tin and peel off the lining paper. Drizzle with a little of the coulis and scatter some raspberries over the top. Serve in slices with the rest of the coulis.

• Per serving 461 kcalories, protein 2g, carbohydrate 23g, fat 39g, saturated fat 24g, fibre 1g, sugar 19g, salt 0.06g

To make this a little boozy, splash a few tablespoons of armagnac or brandy over the fruit before grilling.

# Sticky Figs with Pistachios

8 ripe figs
large knob of butter
4 tbsp clear honey
4–5 tbsp brandy
good handful of shelled pistachio nuts or almonds
1 tsp ground cinnamon or mixed spice
mascarpone cheese or thick Greek yoghurt, to serve

Takes 10 minutes • Serves 4

1 Pre-heat the grill to medium high. Cut a deep cross in the top of each fig then ease the top apart like a flower.
2 Sit the figs in a baking dish and drop a small piece of the butter into the centre of each fruit. Drizzle the honey over the figs, then the brandy. Scatter over the nuts and spice.
3 Grill for 5 minutes until the figs are softened and the honey and butter make a sticky sauce in the bottom of the dish. Serve warm, with dollops of mascarpone or yoghurt.

• Per portion 222 kcalories, protein 3.7g, carbohydrate 25.1g, fat 8.9g, saturated fat 2.6g, fibre 1.8g, sugar 23.9g, salt 0.07g

The ideal no-cook end to a dinner party: this perfect combination of a divine dessert, coffee and Vin Santo is simple to prepare.

# Chocolate Creams with Espresso and Vin Santo

250g carton mascarpone cheese
4 tsp icing sugar
200g/8oz fresh vanilla custard from 500g pot
25g/1oz plain chocolate, grated
zest 1 orange

TO SERVE
6 cups strong espresso or very strong coffee
37.5cl bottle Vin Santo (enough for 6 glasses)
250g pack cantuccini biscotti (little, hard, Italian almond biscuits)

Takes 10 minutes • Serves 6

1  Tip the mascarpone into a bowl and beat with a wooden spoon to soften. Add the icing sugar and custard, stirring until smooth.
2  Fold in the chocolate and orange zest. Spoon into six small glasses, cover and chill until needed.
3  When ready to serve, prepare the coffee. Serve the coffee alongside the chocolate creams, with a glass of Vin Santo and biscuits for dipping.

• Per serving 263 kcalories, protein 3g, carbohydrate 13g, fat 23g, saturated fat 14g, fibre none, sugar 10g, salt 0.15g

A fragrant delight for a hot summer's day that is gentle on the taste-buds as well as the waistline.

# Baked Peaches with Rosewater

6 ripe peaches, halved and stoned
juice 1 large orange
2 tbsp rosewater
100g/4oz golden caster sugar
2 cinnamon sticks, broken
vanilla ice cream, to serve

Takes 30 minutes • Serves 6

1  Pre-heat the oven to 220°C/Gas 7/fan 200°C. Arrange the peaches cut-side up in a large, shallow, heatproof dish so they fit quite snugly.
2  Mix together the orange juice and rosewater, pour it over the peaches, then sprinkle generously with the sugar.
3  Add the cinnamon and bake for 20 minutes, until the peaches are tender. Alternatively, wrap the peaches in a big foil parcel and cook on the barbecue. Serve warm or chilled with vanilla ice cream.

• Per serving 106 kcalories, protein 1g, carbohydrate 27g, fat none, saturated fat none, fibre 2g, sugar 27g, salt 0.01g

Spanish turrón or nougat made from almonds and honey adds sweetness. Look for top-grade Supreme, almost two-thirds almonds.

# Nougat Ice Cream with Sultanas in Sherry

**FOR THE SAUCE**
250ml/9fl oz very sweet sherry, such as Pedro Ximénez or oloroso
50g/2oz sultanas

**FOR THE ICE CREAM**
500ml/18fl oz full-fat milk
1 vanilla pod, split lengthways
6 egg yolks
284ml carton whipping cream, softly whipped
140g/5oz soft Spanish nougat, such as Jijona turrón, crumbled into bite-sized pieces

Takes 20 minutes, plus 2 days for soaking sauce and freezing ice cream
Serves 6

1  Pour the sherry into a bowl, add sultanas, cover and leave to soak for 1–2 days.
2  Pour the milk into a pan, scrape in the vanilla seeds and add the pod. Warm the milk gently. Whisk the egg yolks in a bowl and pour in the warm milk. Beat and return to the pan. Stir over a gentle heat for 3–4 minutes to thicken slightly. Pour into a bowl, cover with plastic film and cool. Stir in the cream and nougat.
3  Use an electric ice-cream maker to make the ice cream, or pour the mixture into a plastic container, cover and freeze for about 2½ hours until almost firm. Mix and return to the freezer for another 2 hours then mix again. Leave overnight to firm up. Transfer the ice cream to the fridge 30 minutes before serving. Serve with the sauce spooned over.

• Per portion 479 kcalories, protein 8.7g, carbohydrate 32g, fat 30.9g, saturated fat 15.8g, fibre 0.2g, sugar 31.9g, salt 0.23g

If you want to get ahead, these delicious confections can be prepared and kept in the fridge for a few hours before baking.

# Squashed Peach and Almond Tarts

100g/4oz ground almonds
100g/4oz butter, softened
1 egg
50g/2oz golden caster sugar
250g/10oz (½ 500g block)
puff pastry
3 peaches, halved, stoned and
thinly sliced

Takes 50 minutes • Serves 4

1 Beat the almonds, butter, egg and half the sugar in a bowl. Roll the pastry to the thickness of a 20p piece. Using a saucer about 13cm/5in in diameter, cut out 4 circles. Put on a baking sheet and spread each with one tablespoon of almond mixture, leaving a border. Arrange the peach slices on top. Chill for at least 10 minutes before baking. Pre-heat the oven to 220°C/Gas 7/fan 200°C.
2 Bake the tarts for 10 minutes, then remove. Sprinkle liberally with the remaining sugar, cover with baking parchment and lay another baking sheet on top. Flip the sheets so that the tarts are upside-down.
3 Bake for 5–10 minutes more, until the pastry is crisp and the peach is sticky and caramelized.

• Per serving 672 kcalories, protein 12g, carbohydrate 44g, fat 51g, saturated fat 20g, fibre 3g, sugar 21g, salt 0.94g

A melt-in-the-mouth boozy pud that makes the perfect end to a dinner for friends.

# Limoncello Plum Tart

500g pack ready-made shortcrust pastry
zest and juice 2 unwaxed lemons
4 tbsp double cream
100g pack ground almonds
200g/8oz golden caster sugar
5 eggs
100g/4oz butter, melted
8 tbsp limoncello liqueur
6 plums, stoned and cut into wedges
icing sugar, to sift

Takes 1–1¼ hours, plus chilling and cooling • Cuts into 12 slices

1  Roll out the pastry and use it to line a loose-bottomed tart tin, 25cm/10in diameter and about 3–4cm/1¼–1½in deep. Chill for at least half an hour.
2  Pre-heat the oven to 180°C/Gas 4/fan 160°C. Line the pastry with foil, fill with baking beans and bake blind for 15 minutes. Remove beans and foil.
3  Put the lemon zest and juice, cream, almonds, sugar, eggs and melted butter in a large bowl and whisk until smooth, then stir in the limoncello. Put the plums in the pastry case then pour the custard mixture over. Bake for about 20–30 minutes until the custard is just set. Allow to cool, then dredge with icing sugar before serving.

• Per slice 924 kcalories, protein 14g, carbohydrate 83g, fat 57g, saturated fat 25g, fibre 4g, sugar 38g, salt 0.86g

This Italian tart is best served cool, as the custard can be a bit runny when hot and straight from the oven.

# Sultana and Pine Nut Tart

100g/4oz sultanas
4 tbsp rum or cognac

FOR THE PASTRY
300g/10oz plain flour
140g/5oz unsalted butter, cut in pieces
50g/2oz icing sugar
1 egg

FOR THE CUSTARD
5 egg yolks
140g/5oz golden caster sugar
284ml carton single cream
½ tsp vanilla extract
85g/3oz pine nuts
icing sugar, for sifting

Takes about 1 hour, plus overnight soaking and 1 hour chilling
Serves 6–8

1 Soak the sultanas in the rum or cognac for 2–3 hours, or preferably overnight.
2 Whiz the flour, butter, icing sugar and egg in a processor to make a dough. Use to line a 25cm/10in flan tin. Freeze for 1 hour. Preheat the oven to 180°C/Gas 4/fan 160°C. Bake the pastry case blind (lined with foil and filled with baking beans) for 10 minutes. Remove the paper and beans.
3 Beat the egg yolks and sugar until pale and thick, but not too foamy. Stir in the cream and vanilla. Drain the sultanas, scatter over the pastry with 50g/2oz of the pine nuts. Pour the custard into the pastry case and bake for 25–30 minutes until the sides look golden. Let it cool, sprinkle with the remaining nuts and dust with icing sugar.

• Per portion 811 kcalories, protein 13g, carbohydrate 87.6g, fat 45.3g, saturated fat 20.9g, fibre 2.2g, sugar 49.4g, salt 0.12g

Crumbling buttery pastry, creamy custard filling and juicy
strawberries can only be a recipe for success.

# Strawberry Vanilla Tart

250g/9oz ready-made sweet
shortcrust pastry

FOR THE CRÈME PÂTISSIÈRE
5 egg yolks
2 tsp vanilla sugar
100g/4oz golden caster sugar
50g/2oz plain flour
425ml/¾ pint milk
25g/1oz butter

TO FINISH
500g/1lb 2oz strawberries, preferably
small, hulled and halved
2 tbsp redcurrant or quince jelly

Takes about 1 hour, plus cooling
Serves 8

1  Pre-heat the oven to 190°C/Gas 5/
fan 170°C. Roll out the pastry and line a
23cm/9in shallow tart tin. Bake with foil and
beans for 10 minutes, then bake the pastry
for another 5 minutes. Let it cool then remove
the pastry from its tin and put on a rack.
2  Whisk the egg yolks, vanilla and sugars
until pale and thick. Whisk in the flour. Boil the
milk then whisk into the egg mixture. Return
to the pan and whisk over a gentle heat.
When thickened, cook for 2 minutes more.
3  Remove from the heat. Beat in the butter.
Spoon into a bowl, cover with cling film
and cool. Set the pastry on a serving plate.
Spread custard over the case almost to fill.
Arrange the strawberries over the custard.
Warm the jelly in a pan with one tablespoon
of water. Brush over the strawberries to glaze.

• Per serving 345 kcalories, protein 6g, carbohydrate
43g, fat 17g, saturated fat 6g, fibre 1g, sugar 26g,
salt 0.30g

*A fresh take on a classic dessert – pastry and fruit make this a mouth-tingling blend of textures.*

# Apricot Crème Brûlée Tart

**FOR THE PASTRY**
140g/5oz butter
100g/4oz golden caster sugar
250g/9oz plain flour
25g/1oz ground almonds
1 egg, beaten

**FOR THE FILLING**
250g pack ready-to-eat dried apricots
175ml/6fl oz sweet dessert wine, such as Sauternes
100g/4oz golden caster sugar, plus 4 tbsp to brûlée
284ml carton double cream
1 vanilla pod, split and seeds scraped
4 eggs, whisked

Takes a staggered 3 hours
Cuts into 10 slices

1 Beat the butter and sugar together until pale then mix in the flour, almonds and egg to make a dough. Wrap and chill for 30 minutes. Put the apricots into a bowl. Bring the wine and sugar to boil, pour over the apricots, set aside. Bring the cream and vanilla to boil. Take off the heat and leave to infuse. Pre-heat the oven to 220°C/Gas 7/fan 200°C.
2 Roll the pastry and line a 23cm/9in fluted tart tin. Freeze for 10 minutes. Bake for 20 minutes with foil and beans, then for 5 minutes without. Remove. Reduce the oven temperature to 160°C/Gas 3/fan 140°C.
3 Strain the vanilla mix over the eggs and whisk. Drain the apricots and stir their liquid into the eggs. Pull the apricots apart and put, sticky sides down, on the pastry. Pour the eggs over. Bake for 30 minutes until just set. Cool. Scatter four tablespoons of sugar over the top and caramelize with a blowtorch.

• Per serving 510 kcalories, protein 8g, carbohydrate 52g, fat 30g, saturated fat 17g, fibre 3g, sugar 20g, salt 0.42g

Polenta and ground almonds replace flour in this all-in-one mixture, to make an amazingly moist cake with a nutty texture.

# Polenta and Almond Cake

225g/8oz softened butter, plus extra for greasing
good pinch of saffron strands
1 tbsp warm water
225g/8oz golden caster sugar
4 medium eggs
½ tsp almond extract
125g/4½oz instant polenta
100g/4oz ground almonds
1½ tsp baking powder
icing sugar, for sifting

Takes 1 hour • Serves 8–12

1  Pre-heat the oven to 180°C/Gas 4/fan 160°C from cold. Butter a 24cm/9½in cake tin, 5cm/2in deep. ILne with baking parchment. Soak the saffron strands in the warm water.

2  Whisk the remaining ingredients, except the icing sugar, with an electric mixer until thoroughly blended, light and fluffy. Strain the saffron water over the mixture, whisk briefly.

3  Pour the mixture into the tin and level the surface. Bake for 45 minutes. Test the cake is cooked by inserting a skewer into the centre – it should come out clean. Let the cake cool in the tin for about 30 minutes, then turn it out and carefully peel off the lining paper. Turn the cake the right way up and put on a wire rack until completely cold. Sift icing sugar all over the cake before serving.

• Per serving for eight 492 kcalories, protein 7g, carbohydrate 44g, fat 33g, saturated fat 6g, fibre 1g, sugar 30g, salt 0.95g

The perfect biscuits to serve with a glass of Moroccan mint tea.

# Sweet Almond Biscuits

1 egg
100g/4oz icing sugar, plus extra
for shaping
1 tsp baking powder
200g pack ground almonds
½ tsp rosewater
12 whole blanched almonds

Takes 30 minutes • Makes 12

1 Pre-heat the oven to 180°C/Gas 4/fan 160°C. Mix all the ingredients except the blanched almonds to make a thick paste.
2 Roll into balls, flatten slightly in icing sugar so they are generously coated, then top with an almond.
3 Place on an oiled baking sheet and bake for 15 minutes until firm and pale golden. Cool on a wire rack.

• Per biscuit 149 kcalories, protein 4g, carbohydrate 10g, fat 10g, saturated fat 1g, fibre 1g, sugar 9g, salt 0.15g

Saffron, citrus fruits and almonds are all of Spanish origin. Here they come together in a mellow yellow cake that has a tangy flavour and a moist texture.

# Spanish Saffron Tea Bread

150ml/¼ pint hot milk
good pinch of saffron strands
175g/6oz butter, cut into pieces, plus extra for greasing
350g/12oz self-raising flour, sifted
100g/4oz ground almonds
140g/5oz golden caster sugar
2 eggs, beaten
grated zest 1 orange and 6 tbsp fresh orange juice (from about 2 oranges)
50g/2oz cut mixed peel
1–2 tbsp clear honey, to glaze

Takes about 1½ hours, plus 1 hour soaking • Cuts into 12 slices

1 Soak the hot milk and saffron strands in a bowl for at least 1 hour. Pre-heat the oven to 170°C/Gas 3/fan 150°C. Butter and line the base of a 25 x 13 x 6cm/10 x 5 x 2½in loaf tin with greaseproof paper.

2 Rub the butter into the flour, stir in the almonds and sugar. Add the beaten eggs, orange zest, orange juice and mixed peel to the saffron milk, mix well. Pour into the flour mixture and beat until evenly mixed. Spoon into the loaf tin and level the surface. Bake for 1–1¼ hours until a skewer inserted in the centre of the cake comes out clean.

3 Leave the bread to cool in the tin for 10 minutes. Turn out on a wire rack and brush the top with honey. When cold, wrap in foil and store in a tin. It is best kept for a couple of days before slicing.

• Per slice 344 kcalories, protein 6g, carbohydrate 41g, fat 18g, saturated fat 9g, fibre 2g, sugar 16g, salt 0.63g

For maximum flavour, use the best plump olives you can in this traditional Italian recipe.

# Olive Bread

650g/1lb 7oz strong plain flour
7g sachet easy-blend yeast
1 tsp fine sea salt
3 tbsp olive oil
250–275ml/9–9½fl oz hand-hot water
140g/5oz black and green olives, pitted (total weight) and chopped

Takes about 1 hour, plus rising • Makes 1 large loaf

1  Mix the flour, yeast, salt and oil in a bowl. Pour in most of the water and mix to a stiff, sticky dough. Add enough water so the dough feels damp. Knead the dough on a lightly floured surface for 10 minutes. Knead in the olives. Put into a lightly oiled bowl. Cover with a clean, damp cloth and let it rise until doubled in size, for 1¼–1½ hours.
2  Punch the dough on the work surface and knead again for 2–3 minutes. Roll it into a 60cm/24in sausage, then fold it loosely in half so it is 30cm/12in long. Twist once. Pinch the ends to seal. Lay the loaf on an oiled baking sheet, cover and let it rise until doubled in size, for 30 minutes. Pre-heat the oven to 200°C/Gas 6/fan 180°C. Just before putting the loaf in the oven, brush with a little water. Bake for 30 minutes until golden.

• Per loaf 2669 kcalories, protein 79g, carbohydrate 490g, fat 58g, saturated fat 8g, fibre 24g, added sugar none, salt 13.07g

# Index

# Picture and recipe credits

*BBC Good Food Magazine* and BBC Books would like to thank the following for providing photographs. While every effort has been made to trace and acknowledge all photographers, we should like to apologize should there be any errors or omissions.

Marie-Louise Avery p141, p193; Steve Baxter p29; Martin Brigdale p25; Peter Cassidy p13, p77, p119, p125, p129, p135; Jean Cazals p57, p111, p133, p145, p205; William Heap p33, p45; William Lingwood p19; Jason Lowe p101; Gareth Morgans p11, p21, p23, p35, p37, p39, p73, p75, p79, p91, p123, p149, p151, p155; David Munns p17, p63, p65, p81, p87, p115, p127, p167, p169, p191; Myles New p147; Mike Pope p179; William Reavell p165; Craig Robertson p27, p71, p103, p183, p189; Maria Jose Sevilla p93, p173, p177; Roger Stowell p97, p117, p121, p137, p139, p143, p175, p181, p201, p211; Simon Walton p195; Fran Warde p99; Cameron Watt p203; Philip Webb p15, p31, p47, p51, p53, p59, p61, p67, p69, p83, p85, p89, p94, p113, p153, p159, p161, p163, p171, p185, p199, p209; Simon Wheeler p41, p43, p157; Kate Whitaker p55, p109; Geoff Wilkinson p131; Anna Venturi

All the recipes in this book have been created by the editorial team on *BBC Good Food Magazine* and regular contributors to the magazine.

Thanks to Mary Cadogan for granting permission to use her recipes for *Lamb Printanière* p174, *Langoustines with Tarragon* p116 and *Pork Terrine with Prosciutto and Oregano* p114.